Becoming a Mensch

Timeless Talmudic Ethics
for Everyone

Ronald Pies

Hamilton Books
A member of
The Rowman & Littlefield Publishing Group
Lanham • Boulder • New York • Toronto • Plymouth, UK

Copyright © 2011 by
Hamilton Books
Copyright © 2011 by
Hamilton Books
4501 Forbes Boulevard
Suite 200
Lanham, Maryland 20706
Hamilton Books Acquisitions Department (301) 459-3366

Estover Road
Plymouth PL6 7PY
United Kingdom

Library of Congress Control Number: 2010931127
ISBN: 978-0-7618-5296-4 (paperback : alk. paper)
eISBN: 978-0-7618-5297-1

∞™ The paper used in this publication meets the minimum
requirements of American National Standard for Information
Sciences—Permanence of Paper for Printed Library Materials,
ANSI Z39.48—1992

Contents

Introduction

[A] mensch is someone to admire and emulate, someone of noble character. The key to being "a real mensch" is nothing less than character, rectitude, dignity, a sense of what is right, responsible, decorous.

—Leo Rosten, The Joys of Yiddish, p. 237

We hear the expression all the time: "He (or She) is a real *mensch!*"

The term "mensch" has passed beyond the realm of Yiddish and Jewish usage, and is now part of the American vernacular. Try Googling the term, and going to any of the more than 53 million websites; or check the *American Heritage Dictionary* (dictionary.com), which now defines "mensch" as "a person having admirable characteristics, such as fortitude and firmness of purpose."

But besides "fortitude and firmness of purpose," what are the "admirable characteristics" of the mensch? And how may we understand these personal traits, in the context of Judaic and rabbinical writing? These questions are at the heart of the present work. Yet my intention in this book is not to create a scholarly tome for rabbinical students or theologians. Rather, it is to help the sincere and earnest reader—of any faith or ethnicity—find the road to *becoming* a mensch! This is not an academic exercise, but a journey of exploration. To accompany the reader on this journey, I have created dozens of modern-day vignettes, aimed at illustrating the ethical issues under discussion in a "real" and immediate way. These personal case histories—often based on composites of various individuals I have known, or treated professionally—are designed to draw out the modern-day implications of the ancient wisdom found in the Talmud. I also provide a variety of rabbinical and scholarly glosses on the points made by the vignettes, so that the reader can put the teachings in a historical context.

Though my own background is in the Jewish faith, this book is intended to aid individuals from any religious faith, or who follow no spiritual tradition at all. Indeed, the reader need not be a "believer" of any kind—whether in organized religion or in God—to find this book a suitable guide for becoming a better person. Furthermore, I have tried to use the term "mensch" in a "gender-neutral" way, as much as possible, so that both men and women will feel welcome in this spiritual journey.

In addition to citing numerous Talmudic and rabbinical sources, I also end each chapter on a "personal" note—presenting some renowned figure from the Talmud by means of a very short biographical vignette. This device is based on my belief that ethical lessons are often best absorbed by seeing how a teaching was actually "lived" by a great rabbi, scholar, or commentator.

At the heart of this book—and of "menschlichkeit" (the quality of being a mensch)—is the concept of *ratzon*. As Eugene Borowitz and Francie Schwartz explain in their excellent book, *The Jewish Moral Virtues*, there is no simple, "bumper sticker" meaning of *ratzon*. The term expresses a range of meanings, including but not limited to: *being congenial; cultivating an easy-going nature; showing good will to others; being amiable; speaking gently to others;* and *being accommodating and conciliatory.* These are all characteristics of the mensch, to be sure: but there are many more, including generosity and charity; self-mastery and self-discipline; humility and flexibility; and respect for self and others. The mensch is also an individual of *obligation*: he or she is obligated to uphold ideals of justice, mercy, prudence, and wisdom. Above all, in my view, the mensch is someone in whom these virtues are expressed *in the right circumstances* and *to the right degree*, depending on the needs of the situation at hand: some circumstances, after all, call for more justice than congeniality, whereas others require mercy tempered by prudence.

In writing this book as a non-theologian, I am deeply indebted to countless rabbis, scholars, commentators, and teachers—not to mention friends, family, and many I have known in my professional capacity as a psychiatric physician. I am especially indebted to the works of Rabbi Joseph Telushkin; Rabbi Byron L. Sherwin; Rabbi Seymour J. Cohen; Rabbi Eugene Borowitz; Rabbi Abraham Yaakov Finkel; and Rabbi Daniel Z. Feldman, for their extraordinarily helpful books and teachings. I also wish to thank Rabbi Steven Carr Rueben, Ph.D., for his encouragement. My esteemed colleagues, Cynthia M.A. Geppert MD, PhD and Dr. Robert Deluty, provided encouragement and comments on an early version of the text. My colleagues at Tufts University School of Medicine, Upstate Medical University, and the *Psychiatric Times* also deserve thanks for encouraging my efforts. Thanks to Chantelle Marshall for her diligent editing. Finally, my wife, Nancy L. Butters, L.C.S.W., has been a constant source of support and inspiration during the writing of this book.

I hope the reader will join the community of ethicists, rabbis, and scholars discussed in this book, who have spent their lives developing and realizing the ideals of the mensch!

A note on references: All quotations from *Pirke Avot* are taken from Rabbi Bulka's translation (Chapters of the Sages, 1993) unless otherwise noted. All Biblical quotations are taken from *The Oxford Annotated Bible, Revised Standard Version* (Oxford University Press, 1962) unless otherwise noted.

Chapter One

A Brief Tour of the Talmudic Territory

It is fair to say that the ethics of Judaism rests atop two gigantic pillars: the *Torah* and the *Talmud*. (Some would add a third pillar: the legal code known as *Shulchan Arukh*, assembled by Rabbi Yosef Karo in the 16th century; see Fogel and Friedman, 2008, 237). The word "Torah" is often translated as "Law," but that term is somewhat inaccurate. "Torah" is derived from the Hebrew *yarah*, meaning "to indicate" or "to instruct" (Biblical Hebrew, n.d.). So, on one level, Torah is essentially the entire repository of ethical "instruction"—including the Talmud—that guides the Jewish people. More concretely, however, *Torah* is usually the name given to the Five Books of Moses (also called *"Chumash," or "Pentateuch,"* which consists of Genesis (Hebrew name: *Bereishis*), Exodus (*Shemos*), Leviticus (*Vayikra*), Numbers (*Bamidbar*), and Deuteronomy (*Devarim*). The term "Torah" is also applied to what is sometimes called the Hebrew Bible or the "Old Testament" (though the latter term is not used in Judaic scholarship). This broader "Torah" includes the aforementioned five books of Moses, the eight books of the *prophets*, and eleven books of the *writings*. These 24 books make up the written law, known collectively as *Tanach*—an acronym formed from letters in the Hebrew words *Torah, Nevi'im* ("Prophets"), and *Ketuvim* ("Writings").

On a more exalted level, Torah is sometimes viewed as the underlying moral structure of the entire Universe! As Adler puts it,

> it was more than a fondness for rhetoric that prompted [the Rabbis] to say that God had looked into the Torah before He began the work of creation. The plan preceded the world which was based upon it...[Torah] is the underlying moral law upon which the Cosmic Lawgiver reared the structure...He had designed (Adler 1963, 98).

You might imagine that, for the Jewish people, no moral teachings could ever surpass Torah, or even complement it in any way. Indeed, if "Torah" is understood broadly enough to include the "oral Torah" —which, in rabbinical tradition, was transmitted to Moses along with the written Torah—this conclusion is warranted. But if we restrict our discussion to the "written Torah"—specifically, to the *Tanach*—it soon becomes clear that something over and above the "letter of the law" was needed. And here we enter the world that preoccupies us for the remainder of this book: the world of *Talmud*.

As Rabbi Morris Adler tell us,

> Divine in origin and character, [the written Torah]...was nonetheless obscure in some places. Its words did not always yield clear directions as to conduct. There were passages of uncertain intent and words whose connotation was not known. Frequently a law or institution was cited in so general a way that the lack of detailed prescription did not indicate the procedure to be followed in its observance...Nor was the Book entirely free from apparent contradictions (Adler 1963, 23).

To deal with these interpretive problems, another process was required, in which the "intent [of the Book], hidden beneath surface discrepancies and perplexities, [would] be brought to light through exploration, patient study, diligent and dedicated probing" (Adler 1963, 24).

This process of study and probing culminated in the creation of the *Mishnah*—the first portion of what we now call the *Talmud*. In modern-day parlance, the *Mishnah* ("Study") might be termed the "user's manual" for the written Torah. As Adler points out, the *Mishnah* was not without controversy and critics; for example, some felt that the oral traditions should not be written down, lest this new "upstart" supplant the Torah itself.

And yet, at the end of the second century C.E., Rabbi Judah Ha-Nasi (the Patriarch) assembled and edited the compilation of the Oral Law—the unwritten teachings that sages had passed along to their students for generations. The *Mishnah* is divided into six main divisions or Orders (in Hebrew, *Shisha Sedarim*, sometimes abbreviated as *Shass*—a term often used as short-hand for Talmud). Each Order is divided into sections called *tractates*, of which there are sixty-three. Each tractate is further divided into chapters (*pirkei*; singular=*perek*). Somewhat confusingly, in the *Mishnah*, each section of a chapter is also referred to as a "Mishnah."

As Adler tells us, the *Mishnah* "gained immediate acceptance as the authoritative work in the field of interpreting and amplifying the contents of Scripture" (Adler 1963, 35). But we should not think of the *Mishnah* as a cut-and-dried list of rabbinical decisions—far from it. Of the 523 chapters contained in the *Mishnah*, only six are free from disagreement between the authorities (Adler 1963, 38)!

The sages of the *Mishnah* are known as *Tannaim* ("teachers"), and are distinguished from later scholars called *Amoraim* ("interpreters"). The *Amoraim* were responsible for what became known as the *Gemara,* which is essentially a commentary on the *Mishnah.* Although the terms *Gemara* and *Talmud* are sometimes used synonymously, we will regard the Talmud as including both the *Mishnah* and the *Gemara* (Adler 1963, 50).

And so, the *Tanach* generated the *Mishnah*, which in turn generated the *Gemara.* As you might anticipate, the more discussion and disagreement, the longer the writing! Thus, the *Mishnah* is several times longer than the Biblical scriptures on which it is based; and the *Gemara* is many times larger than the *Mishnah* (Adler, 1963, 50).

Throughout this book, the reader will find references to either the "Palestinian" (Jerusalem) Talmud, or the "Babylonian" Talmud. This reflects the twin geographical and historical processes that, in effect, generated two closely related Talmuds. The sages in Babylonia (near present-day Iraq) worked in towns such as Pumbeditha and Sura, and were mainly students of Rabbi Judah Ha-Nasi. The most noted of these early Babylonian teachers (*amoraim*) were Rab (Rava) and Samuel (Shmuel). There were close relations between the sages in Babylonia and those in Palestine, and the two Talmuds were edited more or less contemporaneously. The Jerusalem Talmud reached fruition roughly around the year 400 C.E.; the Babylonian Talmud, around 500 C.E. (Elkins 2007, xv). Both Talmuds are based on the same *Mishnah*, but differ in the *Gemara.* The Babylonian Talmud (sometimes called "Bavli") is larger, better edited, and generally considered more authoritative than the Palestinian Talmud (Adler 1963, 55).

Each Talmud contains both legal (*Halachic*) and non-legal (*Aggadic*) material. (The term "Aggadah"—roughly, folklore and moral aphorisms—is sometimes rendered as "Haggadah.") The Aggadic material is of special interest to us, since many of the purely ethical teachings of the Talmud are contained in its Aggadic portions. But, as Adler notes, there is no wall of separation between law and ethics in Judaism; on the contrary, "Jewish ethics are impressed upon the *Halacha* [law], as well as expressed in the *Haggada.*" Indeed, "Law in Judaism...is in the last analysis the instrument of religion and ethics" (Adler 1963, 65–66). We might say, on another level, that "The relentless passion of the Jewish people has been about how to grow the soul" (Elkins 2007, xvii). This spiritual growth occurs through understanding and living out both *Halacha* and *Haggada*—and is the driving force behind "becoming a mensch."

Undoubtedly the best-known Aggidic portion (or Tractate) of the Talmud is known as *Pirkei Avos* (or *Pirke Avot*), which—roughly and variously translated—means "Chapters of the Sages" or "Ethics of the Fathers." Pirke Avot is unique among the tractates of the Talmud, since it is the only tractate that deals exclusively with the moral and ethical lessons of the Sages. Pirke Avot was compiled by the same Rabbi Judah Ha-Nasi we discussed earlier. It consists of the favorite maxims of some 60 Rabbis, covering a period from roughly 300 B.C.E. to 200 C.E., as well as some anonymous sayings and folkloric themes. Traditionally, *Pirkei* was part of the Sabbath prayer book (*Siddur*), and it is said to have been a favorite of students during the summer months.

By now, the reader may have concluded that Torah and Talmud are really texts meant only for Jews—but that would be a distinctly "un-Jewish" conclusion! The philosopher Rabbi Leo Baeck (1873–1956) pointed out (Adler 1963, 99) that nowhere in the Hebrew Bible or later rabbinical writings does the term "good Jew" occur. Rather, it is the "good man" (and good woman) who is the object of ethical concern—the individual we call the *mensch.* Adler notes that Torah is understood as "a moral law that is binding upon all mankind" (Adler, 1963, p. 99). This claim may not sit well with some individuals steeped in other religious traditions. And yet, as I have suggested in another book (Pies 2000), there is much common ground between the ethical principles of Judaism and those of the world's other major faiths (Buddhism, Islam, Christianity, and Hinduism). Indeed, I would argue that the moral teachings of Torah and Talmud are of crucial importance to anyone—of *any faith* or of *no faith*—who wants to become a mensch!

Chapter Two

Kindness and Compassion

For I desire kindness, not sacrifice.

—Hosea 6:6, speaking in the name of God

The world stands on three things—on the Torah, on the Sacred Service, and on the practice of loving-kindness.

— Shimon the righteous, Pirke Avot 1:2

A religious [individual] is a person ...whose greatest passion is compassion [and] whose greatest strength is love and defiance of despair.

—Rabbi Abraham Joshua Heschel

What do we live for if it is not to make life less difficult for each other?

—George Eliot

Rabbi Abraham Joshua Heschel (1907–1972) once said, "When I was young I admired clever people. Now that I am old, I admire kind people" (Telushkin 1994, 182). Indeed, as Rabbi Joseph Telushkin suggests, kindness and compassion compose the keystone in the great arch of Jewish values. In a sense, all other Jewish values depend on, and may be derived from, these central virtues, which are expressed in Hebrew by the word *rahamim*. Thus, Rabbi Shlomo Toperoff tells us that, "Torah itself cannot exist if it is divorced from acts of loving-kindness" (Toperoff 1997, 25).

Another way of putting it: without kindness and compassion, no matter what else you do in life, you are not a mensch, and you are not living like a worthy and decent human being. Indeed, the Talmud tells us, "one who shows no pity for fellow creatures is assuredly not of the seed of Abraham,

5

our father" (Babylonian Talmud, Betzah 32a; cited in Telushkin 1994, 182). A consistently unkind person is, spiritually speaking, essentially expelled from the Jewish community. I would argue that such a person is not fit to be a member of the *human* community—while adding the caveat that we are all capable of changing for the better, and that even habitually unkind people should not be "written off" as beyond redemption. (That would be neither kind nor compassionate!) Let's see how the qualities of kindness and compassion are sometimes put to the test:

There was no love lost between Carol and Malkah, her mother-in-law. " 'Malkah' means "Queen", doesn't it?" Carol would tease her husband, Joel. "Well, your mother sure lives up to the billing!" It was true that Malkah criticized Carol at almost every opportunity, though she (Malkah) "meant well." Usually, Malkah's critiques were in the nature of "looking out for my son," and involved such things as how Carol would prepare meals, whether she was spending enough time with Joel, etc. Occasionally, though, Malkah would rip into Carol for no apparent reason. Once, Malkah made the statement, "Joel would have been better off if he had never married, the way you treat him!" This jibe had hurt Carol deeply, and she had never fully forgiven Malkah for the remark. One night, Carol and Joel received a phone call from Joel's father, who was calling from the hospital. Malkah had suffered a mild stroke, and was having trouble with arm movement and speech. She was expected to recover, but would need a lot of "rehab" and assistance at home. Carol began to wonder what her responsibilities were, given how Malkah had treated her.

We will have more to say later, regarding a child's responsibilities to his or her parents (and in-laws!), as well the mutual responsibilities involved in "forgiveness." (Forgiveness is not a one-way street, as we shall see.) But for now, it's enough to say that Talmudic ethics call for kindness and compassion at this point in Carol's life—notwithstanding Malkah's own less-than-spotless record of kindness. In a situation like this, it is Carol's responsibility to let her "good inclination" (*yetzer tov*) overcome her "evil inclination" (*yetzer hara*), and to assist her mother-in-law as best she can. Ideally, Carol would find a way to do this without a sense of disgruntled and begrudging duty—though this would hardly be easy! But, as Borowitz and Schwartz put it, "Only when we find the inner power to lovingly take back the one who hurt us can we overcome estrangement" (Borowitz and Schwartz 1999, 69).

How does a person who has been hurt by another find the ability to show *rahamim* to that individual? One way is suggested by Rabbi Zelig Pliskin, who describes a group in Israel that meets on a regular basis, and actually

tries to come up with "excuses" for slights that group members have suffered! As quoted by Rabbi Joseph Telushkin (2000, 35), here is one example:
You were hoping that somebody would invite you to his house, but he failed to do so.

a. Perhaps someone in his family is ill.
d. Perhaps he was planning to be away from home.
c. Perhaps he did not have enough food in his house.

So, in the case of Carol and Malkah, perhaps Carol might come up with a few creative "excuses" for Malkah's inconsiderate behavior; for example, "Maybe Malkah needs to criticize me because she is afraid she *herself* hasn't done enough for Joel. Or, maybe she doesn't know how to express affection, except by criticizing." Sure, these may sound like "lame" rationalizations, and they are *not* meant to exonerate Malkah. But for the moment—and particularly in the circumstances of Malkah's stroke—inventing some plausible "excuses" for Malkah's bad behavior will do more good than harm. They may allow Carol to get in touch with her "better angels" (*yetzer tov*) and show compassion to her mother-in-law.

Kindness and compassion don't always involve a "positive" intervention in the life of another, such as sending flowers to a hospitalized friend. Sometimes *rachamim* involves *removing some obstacle* that could harm or thwart another. In the Old Testament, we are told, "Don't put a stumbling block in front of a blind man" (Leviticus 19:14). But it is not enough to refrain from such obvious cruelty; we must also *remove* "stumbling blocks" that endanger, hamper, or in any way diminish the well-being of others (Telushkin 2000, 297).

Bruce was an "up and coming" young executive at a computer software company. He had been with the company for ten years, and had put his heart and soul into his work. Bruce was up for promotion to Senior Vice President, but so was Rita, a long-time colleague and friend. Bruce and Rita had always been respectful of one another, even as they competed for various positions within the company. Two days before both Bruce and Rita were to have an important interview with the CEO of the company, Bruce discovered that an e-mail from an important client—intended for Rita—had somehow come to him. Before realizing that the message was not meant for him (it began, "Hi, I thought you'd like to know that I was very impressed with your presentation..."), Bruce read the contents of the message. The client's e-mail reflected very favorably upon Rita and her work in behalf of the company. For a few

minutes, Bruce debated whether he should alert Rita to the error—or do noth-
ing. If Bruce did nothing—or simply deleted the message—Rita might never
know how favorably impressed the client was with her and might never be
able to use that information in her own behalf, as she competed for the Senior
V.P. position. If Bruce did alert Rita to the error, he could risk putting himself
at a relative disadvantage, with respect to the promotion.

What are Bruce's obligations under the ethics of the Torah and Talmud? First, it's important to note that Judaism generally views spiritual or material success (in Hebrew, *hatzlachah*) as a blessing. But, as Rabbi Louis Jacobs reminds us, "Success is a good provided it is not seen as self-made but as God-made, and is not attained *through disregard for the interests of others*" (Jacobs 1999, 243, italics added).

In the case at hand, Rita was "blind" to the "stumbling block" in the path of her career (the missing message). Even if it means Bruce's losing an advantage in his competition with Rita, he is morally obligated to notify her of the missed e-mail message. That's just part of being a mensch! In one sense, this falls under the rubric of "kindness." On a more practical level, Bruce's obligation is simply part of honest business practices. As Rabbi David Golinkin puts it:

> the law of the stumbling block can be readily applied to modern situations: a real
> estate agent should not dupe a young couple into buying a home with structural
> faults simply in order to make a fast buck. A stockbroker should not sell his
> client a bad investment just to collect the commission. A salesman should not
> convince his customer to buy an expensive item he really has no use for. These
> are all considered "a stumbling block before the blind" about which we are
> warned "and you shall fear your God, I am the Lord (Golinkin 2002).

In short, we are being honest and ethical both when we do not put a stumbling block before someone who can't "see" the situation clearly, and when we actively *remove* a stumbling block. Both of these small kindnesses are part of what a real mensch does!

The Talmud is filled with other examples of what is called *gemilut hasadim*—acts of loving-kindness. Rabbi Ben Zion Bokser (2001) lists the following as examples:

• Visiting the sick
• Providing hospitality to strangers
• Caring for the orphaned
• Relieving the poor in their distress

The last item requires a bit of clarification. The Rabbis distinguished between *acts of loving-kindness* (benevolence), on the one hand, and *charity* or *almsgiving*, on the other: "Greater is the benevolence than alms," we are told, because "almsgiving is restricted to the poor [whereas] benevolence applies to the poor as well as to the affluent" (Sukkah 49b; cited in Bokser 2001, 131). We will say much more about charity in Chapter 3.

PERSONAL ENCOUNTER: WHAT CHARACTER TRAIT OF THE MENSCH IS THE MOST COMPREHENSIVE? RABBI YOCHANAN'S ANSWER

In the only purely "ethical" work in the Talmud, known as *The Ethics of the Sages* (Pirke Avot 2:13), we read of a certain Rabbi Yochanan, who sent his disciples out to answer the most fundamental of all moral questions: *what is the right path in life?* ("Go forth and see which is the good way to which a person should cleave.") Rabbi Yochanan bar Nafcha (d. 279 C.E.) was one of the most esteemed figures in all of Talmudic literature, famous not only for his wisdom but also for his extraordinary beauty. And yet, his life was one of great sorrow: he had ten sons, all of whom died within his own lifetime. Legend has it that he carried with him a small bone from the body of his tenth son, and would show it to anyone who complained of his fate, saying, "This is the bone of my tenth son" (Berachot 5b; in Steinsaltz 1997, 116).

Rabbi Yochanan's five disciples—Rabbis Eliezer, Yehoshua, Yose, Shimon, and Elazar—apparently did go forth, and must have done some extensive soul-searching. When they returned, here is how each answered the master's question regarding the right path in life. From their answers, it seems clear that the disciples defined the "good way" in terms of *personal qualities*. In effect, they seem to be answering the question, "What is the single character trait that best defines a real mensch?": "R. Eliezer says—A good eye; R. Yehoshua says—A good friend; R. Yose says—A good neighbor; R. Shimon says—One who foresees that which will be; R. Elazar says—A good heart. He (Rabban Yochanan) said to them: I prefer the words of Elazar the son of Arach to yours, for your words are included in his words" (Bulka 1993, 75).

Commenting on this portion of Pirke Avot, Rabbi Reuven Bulka explains this teaching as follows: "A person with a good heart has a good eye, is a good friend and neighbor, and sees the consequences of actions. A good heart feeds sustenance to an entire body; a good heart feeds feeling to an entire community" (Bulka 1993, 76).

Chapter Three

Generosity and Charity

…if someone comes to you and asks your help, you shall not turn him off
with pious words, saying: "Have faith and take your troubles to God!" You
shall act as if there were no God, as if there were only one person in all the
world who could help this man—only yourself.

—Rabbi Moshe Lieb of Sasov, quoted by Martin Buber;
in Besserman 1994, 217

May God save me from the stingy of heart!

—From a Yiddish prayer;
in Borowitz and Schwartz 1999, 94

If your enemy is hungry, give him bread to eat; and if he is thirsty, give
him water to drink.

—Proverbs 25:21

In this chapter, we are concerned with two closely related traits or habits of
the mensch: generosity (*nedivut*) and charity (*tzedakah*). Clearly, there is no
bright line between these attributes and the traits of *kindness and compassion*
we have just reviewed, although in theory they are distinguishable. We might
say roughly that generosity and charity constitute two forms of kindness,
compassion, or good-heartedness.

But before proceeding, we need to take a closer look at the Hebrew word
tzedakah. Our English word "charity" is derived from the Latin *caritas*,
meaning "from the heart." On the other hand, as Rabbi Telushkin points out,
the word *tzedakah* is derived from *tzedek*, meaning "justice." So, *tzedakah*
is much more than just dropping a dollar into the slot of the Salvation Army

kettle. As Telushkin says, "one who gives *tzedakah is* acting justly, while one who doesn't is acting unjustly." Indeed, he continues, "Jewish law regards withholding *tzedakah* as not only ugly but also illegal" (Telushkin 2000, 74). Let's see how such ancient ethical principles come up against the "realities" of our own age.

Lucinda was down on her luck. She had just been laid off from her job as a legal secretary, and she was having trouble making payments on her home mortgage. With three children to feed, and a husband just scraping by doing occasional carpentry work, Lucinda was feeling depressed and anxious. She had just learned that only $1500 remained in her savings account, and that another mortgage payment of $1000 was due in two weeks. And as if this weren't enough, her small Tennessee town had just been hit by a vicious "twister," which had destroyed nearly a quarter of the town. Fortunately, Lucinda's home was spared. Her neighbors had just started taking up a collection for those less fortunate—particularly those who had lost their homes in the tornado. One of her neighbors, Annie, came to Lucinda's door and asked, "Is there any way you could make a small contribution to the neighborhood relief fund, Lucinda?"

What are Lucinda's obligations under Talmudic ethical principles? What would a mensch do in these circumstances? Is somebody in Lucinda's dire financial straits obligated to go into hock, in order to aid her even less fortunate neighbors?

Talmudic ethics are very clear on this point: Lucinda is morally obligated to do what she can, within her means, and contribute *something* to Annie's fund—even if it's just a dollar. Jewish law eventually decreed that Jews should donate at least ten percent of their annual net income to the needy (Telushkin 2000, 75). Even a beggar is required to do whatever he can, by way of *tzedakah*. The Talmud tell us, "If a man sees that his livelihood is barely sufficient for him, he should [still] give charity from it" (Gittin 7a; in Rosenberg 2003, 129); and, "Even a poor man who himself survives on charity should give charity" (Gittin 7b; in Rosenberg 2003, 129). There is a special mitzvah that arises in celebration of Purim, called *matanos l'evyonim* (gifts to the poor), and here we are told to give with special generosity.

On the other hand, Judaic ethics does not require a person to go into bankruptcy or become so destitute from giving charity that his or her family is imperiled. Indeed, in Deuteronomy 4:15, we are told, "You shall carefully preserve your lives"—that surely includes preserving the well-being of your loved ones. As Rabbi Telushkin puts it, "there is such a thing as being too generous…what Judaism particularly esteems is a life of passionate moderation" (Telushkin 2000, 336–7).

Mike was walking through a busy city square one day, when a shabbily dressed figure approached him. "Got any spare change?" came the familiar question. The man certainly looked down on his luck. His clothes were tattered, and he wore a straggly beard that seemed encrusted with some kind of dried liquid. Mike was about to reach into his pocket to pull out a few coins, when he noticed that the man was also wearing what looked like a rather expensive gold chain. Immediately, Mike felt "conflicted." As he put it when discussing the issue with his wife, "I thought maybe this guy was a con artist, or maybe a drug dealer. How do you wind up with a gold chain like that, begging on the street? It didn't make sense." Somewhat reluctantly, Mike gave the man a dollar, but said nothing to him, avoided eye contact, and quickly walked away.

Was Mike acting like a mensch? What does the Talmud tell us about our obligations to provide *tzedakah* in cases of this sort—in which we have serious doubts about the "legitimacy" of the person asking for our help?

Overall, Mike didn't quite rise to the occasion, though he did partially fulfill the "mitzvah" (commandment) of providing sustenance to the poor. The Talmud takes a balanced and sensible approach to the kind of situation Mike faced. It says, "When a man says, 'Provide me with clothes,' he should be investigated (lest he be found to be a cheat); [but] when he says, 'Feed me,' he should not be investigated [but fed immediately, lest he starve to death during the investigation]" (Bava Bathra 9a; as translated by Telushkin 2000, 13).

In the case of Mike's "Got any spare change?" scenario, though, the "beggar" did not indicate that he was hungry, and, indeed, seemed to have the means of providing sustenance to himself—after all, he could have pawned the gold chain. But let's imagine for a minute the not implausible scenario that the man might have been suffering from some kind of mental illness. (Many individuals with chronic schizophrenia find themselves on the street in such dire circumstances.) Perhaps the man was not thinking rationally about pawning the chain. Or maybe the chain had some strong sentimental value to him—perhaps it was the one possession he had managed to salvage from a home (or a relationship) that he had lost. Here, I think, one best serves the spirit of the Talmud by "inventing excuses," as we saw in the previous chapter. What's the worst that could happen if you give such a man a dollar and it turns out he is defrauding you? Yes, he *might* use the dollar to buy alcohol or drugs—but then again, he might be hungry and use it to buy a loaf of bread. (It may be less humiliating for some people on the street to spout the familiar, "Got any spare change?" than to say, "Please, I'm hungry, help feed me!") I would be inclined to give such an unfortunate person the benefit of the doubt, as Mike evidently did. Rabbi Telushkin, in this regard, quotes the Chassidic rebbe, Chaim of Sanz (d. 1786), who said: "The merit of charity is so great that I am happy to give to one hundred beggars even if only one might actually be needy" (Telushkin 2000, 13).

There is one sense, though, in which Mike did not properly carry out the commandment of *tzedakah*. Mike turned away from the beggar, refusing to make eye contact, and said nothing. While understandable, this is nevertheless a violation of Talmudic ethics. As Maimonides put it in his *Mishneh Torah [Laws of Gifts to the Poor]* 10:4: "Whoever gives charity to a poor man ill-manneredly and with downcast looks has lost all the merit of his action even though he gives him a thousand gold pieces. He should give…with good grace and with joy and should sympathize with [the beggar] in his plight" (quoted in Telushkin 2000, 12).

Similarly, as Rabbi Morris Adler puts it, "He who speaks kindly words to the needy is more blessed than he who gives alms unaccompanied by kind words" (Adler 1963, 106).

There is a larger point to be made regarding "charity." As important as it is to help poor people with a monetary gift, it is more praiseworthy (and productive) to help the poor person get "back on her feet." A well-known Chinese proverb says, "Give a man a fish and you feed him for a day. Teach a man to fish and you feed him for a lifetime" (Tripp 1970, 76). Judaic ethics takes a similar position. In his *Mishneh Torah*, Maimonides noted that in the highest degrees of charity, one provides the destitute person with a loan; enters into a business partnership with him or her; or puts the person "in a position where he can dispense with other people's aid" (quoted in Telushkin 2000, 55). An indirect way of accomplishing a similar goal is to start, or contribute to, a scholarship fund for worthy but indigent recipients.

Michelle was in a quandary. She had been contacted by a major funding organization devoted to fighting breast cancer—a cause that Michelle strongly supported, having survived breast cancer herself. Michelle felt ambivalent because she was suspicious of her own motives. "I had planned to give a large sum—around $1000—to this organization. Then I realized that half the reason I was doing so was the thrill I would get from seeing my name printed in this organization's monthly magazine, listed in their 'Angels' category of big donors! I was ashamed of myself for having this tacky, narcissistic motive. I began to think, maybe it would be better not to donate at all, with that kind of selfish attitude."

Should Michelle forget about making this contribution? From the standpoint of Judaic ethics, the clear answer is no. Despite her mixed reasons for giving, Michelle should "be a mensch" and make the donation. It is true that the

Talmud generally likes people to perform acts of kindness and *tzedakah* from "pure" and altruistic motives, such as the wish to benefit humanity. Indeed, in Pirke Avot (5:16), we find a catalogue of "pure" and "impure" motives for giving charity:

> There are four types among givers of charity: One who desires to give but that others should not give—begrudges what belongs to others; one who desires that others should give but he not give—begrudges what belongs to himself; one who desires to give and that others should give—this characterizes the pious person; one who does not give and desires that others should not give—this characterizes the wicked person.

Furthermore, tact and discretion in giving alms is a hallmark of Judaism. Thus, Rabbi Eliezer states, "He who ostentatiously gives alms to the poor—for this, God will bring him to judgment" (Hagigah 5a; as translated by Newman and Spitz 1945, 62). Nevertheless—and notwithstanding the importance of motive—Judaism still holds that *charity is worthwhile in its own right*; for even if one's motives are not "pure," the poor are nevertheless sustained by the act of giving (Besserman 1994, 125).

Ben's second cousin, Morty, was known in the family as a "schnorrer"— roughly translated, a "mooch." In the colorful description by Jacobs and Eisenstein (n.d.), a schnorrer is

> a Jewish beggar having some pretensions to respectability. In contrast to the ordinary house-to-house beggar, whose business is known and easily recognized, the schnorrer assumes a gentlemanly appearance, disguises his purpose, gives evasive reasons for asking assistance, and is not satisfied with small favors, being indeed quite indignant when such are offered.

Morty truly was impoverished. He had been down on his luck for the last ten years, owing to a combination of poor planning, laziness, and some genuinely bad breaks in the job market. Recently, Morty had tried, unsuccessfully, to start his own consulting business, but apparently, few people believed that Morty could provide expert consultation in the area of "estate planning," for which he had essentially no professional training. ("That's not true," Morty told Ben. "I took a correspondence course!") One day, Morty literally showed up on Ben's doorstep, carrying a battered suitcase and a grocery bag full of assorted papers. "Here's the thing, Ben," Morty began, "I'm trying to finish an article for the New York Times, and I need a place to crash for a few days— you know, just to get away from all the distractions at my place." In truth, Morty didn't have "a place," and been sleeping in bus stations and airports for the past month. Ben felt a terrible sinking feeling in the pit of his stomach

as soon as he heard Morty's story. "I knew I was in deep trouble if I said yes,"
Ben later explained to his wife. "But I felt like I couldn't say no, either."

What are Ben's (and his wife's) responsibilities in relation to poor Morty? What does a mensch do when faced with anyone who is impoverished, down on his luck, and in need of a home? In Pirke Avot (1:5), we read as follows: "Yose the son of Yochanan, of Jerusalem, says: Let your house be opened wide, let the poor be members of your household…"

And in another portion of the Talmud, we find the following: "R. Yohanan said: Extending hospitality to strangers is as great as attending the academy, for the Mishnah likens making room for guests to removing an impediment in the academy" (Shabbat 127a-127b; quoted in Bokser 1989, 94).

But how do we translate these noble principles into guidelines for our own time? It hardly seems reasonable, in this day and age, to literally leave the doors of our houses open to indigent strangers, or to take in such persons directly off the street. It seems unlikely that the Rabbis of the Talmudic era— who were, by and large, eminently practical men—could have intended such potentially dangerous behaviors. Rather, the Rabbis were intent on creating an *attitude and orientation* toward the poor and needy: one of open-heartedness, acceptance, and respect. But attitude alone is not enough. We must convert the attitude into action. Thus, Rabbi Bulka says we must ensure that "those who come to you for material or spiritual help do not feel like strangers in an alien environment, but like members of the house" (Bulka 1993, 29). So, we must go out of our way to help the needy without patronizing or humiliating them. If the circumstances permit us to do so *safely*, we should open our house and home to the needy with warmth and understanding. Similarly, Rabbi Toperoff notes the importance of restoring to the poor "his personality and individuality," adding, "do not offer him the crumbs of your table," but rather, "offer him the comforts he was accustomed to enjoy in the past. Such help is not merely charity, but zedakah, a form of righteousness which should be the basis of all charity" (Toperoff 1997, 36).

Ben and his wife clearly have an ethical obligation to assist Morty—not only because he is needy, but because he is also *part of their family*. Indeed, the great medieval ethicist, Jacob ben Asher (d. 1340), notes that *needy relatives must take priority* over others, when it comes to giving charity (see Borowitz and Schwartz 1999, 124–5). And yet: we must also bear in mind the earlier dictum, "When a man says, 'Provide me with clothes,' he should be investigated (lest he be found to be a cheat)." How do we balance this with the need to open our hearts and homes to the needy? There is no pat formula, and the situation becomes more complex with people like Morty, who are known to have a checkered history. Here is how Ben and his wife dealt with the issue:

We agreed to take Morty in, letting him know in advance that he was welcome to stay with us for a few weeks. We felt we needed to give him a rough time frame, because we didn't want to create the expectation that the invitation was open-ended. That would be just too much for Miriam and me, since we tend to be fairly private people. We gave Morty the guest bedroom and didn't ask him any questions about his circumstances for the first few days. We pretty much took his "New York Times article" story at face value and didn't interrogate him. Morty ate his meals with us, we reminisced about old times, and we really tried to treat him like one of the family. I even got the two of us tickets for a Red Sox game. After a couple of weeks, though, it was pretty clear that Morty was not only not working on an article, he wasn't doing much of anything! He would lie around the house most of the day, then borrow my car and drive out to the coffee shop for donuts. Once he came back with alcohol on his breath. At that point, my wife and I felt we needed to have a long talk with Morty. We tried our best to be kind and non-accusatory. We explained that while we loved him, we wanted our "old lives" back, and that Morty would need to move on. I decided to float him a loan at no interest, and gave him a couple of business contacts that might help him get back on his feet. I also drove him around town to look at some low-income apartments. Eventually, we were able to get him settled in a few miles from us, and Morty found some part-time work doing landscaping.

Overall, Ben and Miriam handled the situation with Morty quite admirably. They behaved like real *menschen*!

Mitch was in a quandary. Over the years, his next-door-neighbor, Fred, had been "a real pain in the tuchas*" as Mitch put it. Fred and his wife would host lavish outdoor parties during the summer and refuse to turn down their very loud music when Mitch complained about it, even at two o'clock in the morning. For many years, Fred had refused to trim the hedges that spilled over his fence and into Mitch's yard, blocking the sun from reaching a portion of Mitch's garden. Once, when Fred's lawn mower broke down, Mitch lent him his own mower, and it was weeks before Fred returned it. Perhaps most infuriating, Fred had refused to cover an old well on his property, and more than once, Mitch's cocker spaniel had come perilously close to falling in. Then, late one night, Mitch and his wife were awakened by the wail of sirens. To their horror, they watched as Fred's house went up in flames—a near-total loss. The firemen barely succeeded in keeping the blaze from spreading to Mitch's house. The following day, Fred knocked on Mitch's door and sheepishly asked if he could use Fred's computer and fax modem, in order to send some documents to his insurance company.*

What are Mitch's obligations in this difficult situation? Should Fred's history of thoughtless, passive-aggressive behavior weigh against Mitch's helping him? What would a mensch do in such circumstances?

In essence, the Talmud calls upon us to heed our "better angels"—our *yetzer tov* (good inclination) rather than our *yetzer hara* (evil inclination). The "reference text" is Bava Mezia 32b, which says: "If a friend requires unloading, and an enemy loading, your first obligation is toward your enemy, in order to subdue your evil inclination." This takes precedence even over relieving the burden of your friend's animal. Telushkin interprets the passage as saying, "if you see a person whom you dislike in a difficult situation, and you are in a position to provide assistance, overcome your evil inclination, break the pattern of enmity, and help him or her out" (Telushkin 2000, 376).

Rabbi Daniel Z. Feldman provides another reason why Mitch is obligated to help Fred: avoiding the dual prohibitions against *nekimah*, or *revenge*; and *netirah*, or *bearing a grudge*. Feldman gives an example from the Talmud (Yoma 23a):

> An individual, wishing to borrow his neighbor's sickle, is rebuffed. The next day, the offending neighbor is now himself in need and asks the rejected party to lend him his scythe. If the latter [party] were to obey his natural instinct to refuse, noting the treatment he himself received, he would be in violation of *nekimah*, of revenge…[furthermore] if he cannot also resist the temptation to add, "I am not like you," as he hands over the scythe, he flouts the injunction of *netirah,* of bearing a grudge (Feldman 1999, 96).

This brings us full circle to one of the quotations at the beginning of this chapter, from Proverbs 25:21: *"If your enemy is hungry, give him bread to eat; and if he is thirsty, give him water to drink."*

PERSONAL ENCOUNTER: HOW DO WE PRIORITIZE CHARITY? THE TEACHINGS OF JOSEPH KARO

Joseph Karo (1488–1575) was one of the most renowned legal scholars in all of Jewish history. Like other rabbinical scholars before him (such as Maimonides), Karo also had strong mystical yearnings. Legend has it that during an "all-nighter" on the holiday of Shavuot, Karo was visited by an angel who perched on his shoulder "and kissed Jewish law into his mouth" (Jewish Virtual Library). Karo is perhaps best remembered as the author of the *Shulchan Aruch*, or Code of Jewish Law. This work became tremendously influential in the Jewish world partly because it was the first such code to be printed on the newly invented printing press!

Here is Joseph Karo's teaching on how we should prioritize *tzedakah*:

A man should give to his relatives...before giving to anyone else...The poor in a man's household come before the poor in the town in which he lives. The poor of the town in which he lives come before the poor of another town, and the poor of the land of Israel come before the poor in lands outside Israel" (Code of Jewish Law, *Yoreh De'ah*, chapter 251, section 3; quoted in Klagsbrun 1980, 333).

Chapter Four

Self-Mastery and Self-Discipline

Ben Zoma says: Who is mighty? One who conquers one's passions, as it is said: "One who is slow to anger is better than the mighty, and one who rules over one's spirit is better than one who conquers a city"

—(Proverbs 16:32), Pirke Avot 4:1

Rabbi Tarfon says: The day is short, the task is great, the workers are lazy, and reward is great, and the Master of the house is insistent.

—Pirke Avot 2:20

The son of Hei Hei says: According to the exertion is the reward.

—Pirke Avot 5:27

Judaism in general and the Talmud in particular place a high value on self-restraint, self-discipline, and diligent labor. The Rabbis are especially keen to mitigate (if not eliminate) the terribly destructive effects of unbridled anger. In Proverbs (14:29), we are taught that, "He who is slow to anger has great understanding, but he who has a hasty temper exalts folly." Indeed, Rabbi Shlomo Toperoff notes that *erekh apayim*—being *slow to anger*—is "one of the thirteen attributes of God" (Toperoff 1997, 280). Similarly, a real mensch does not explode at others or yield to rage.

The mensch is also expected to restrain and regulate other strong emotions or desires. In general, Judaism emphasizes *redirecting* rather than *extirpating* passions. Passion "should be mastered, not destroyed" (Lieber 1995, 213). As Unterman puts it, "Instead of the extirpation of desire, Judaism demands a more complicated and problematical achievement—that man, by dint of his will, discipline his desire—that everything be held within proper limits by control and will power" (Unterman, 1964, 214). Thus, "sexuality…is not repressed or denied but is channeled positively within marriage" (Katz and Schwartz 1997, 73). And even within marriage, Maimonides insists that a man should not "be with his wife like a rooster" (*Laws Concerning Character Traits*; cited in Weiss and Butterworth 1983, 42).

Anger, however, is dealt with somewhat ambivalently in the rabbinical tradition. The Vilna Gaon believed that anger "must be totally eradicated, as it has almost no redeeming value" (Lieber 1995, 213). But the word "almost" is important here. Maimonides, in the *Mishneh Torah* (Twersky 1972, 54) describes anger as "an exceedingly bad passion, and one should avoid it to the last extreme." And yet, even Rambam notes the occasional value of *simulating* anger, as when one wants to discipline one's children—so long as one "does not really feel" anger. Thus, Maimonides seems to say that anger is not an *inherently evil* emotion; but rather, a passion *to be bridled and mastered* so that one doesn't truly "feel" it. Notably, Pirke Avot does not admonish us, "Never get angry!" Rather, Ben Zoma urges us to be "*slow* to anger," and Rabbi Eliezer instructs us, "do not anger *easily*" (Pirke Avot 2:15). Indeed, Lieber wisely observes,

> It is really impossible never to get angry, so the mishnah (Pirke Avot 2:15) instructs us not to anger *easily*. We must be level-headed enough to assess whether the incident that sparked our anger is sufficient cause for an outburst. We should actively attempt to *find reasons* not to be angry (Lieber 1995, 106).

Even in those rare circumstances when it may be a *mitzvah* (commandment) to show anger—for example, when there is a public breach of the law—our expression of anger "should be done like all other *mitzvos*—calmly and with much forethought" (Lieber 1995, 106). In short: the mensch has the complicated task of showing, at most, a highly refined and nearly "rational" form of anger! This is clearly not an easy line to walk.

Michelle was an attractive, 38–year-old mother of two who had just been promoted at work. Having struggled for many years in the "boys' club" world of a major Boston law firm, Michelle had just been made a partner in the firm. She was "riding on air" for several weeks, until her first meeting with the head of the firm, a man in his mid-60s whom Michelle described as "kind of a lech" (as in lecher*). Mr. Forbes was known for his patronizing and sometimes inappropriate behavior toward young female partners in the firm. When, during their meeting, Mr. Forbes put his hand on Michelle's knee and suggested that "Your new position will go much more smoothly if we can put you in the right position," Michelle was understandably enraged and appalled, but kept control of her emotions. She calmly removed the boss's hand from her knee, smiled tightly, and said simply, "Mr. Forbes, I want to do a* *good job for this firm. I hope you'll let me do that by showing me the same respect you show to all the new partners. Now, sir, if you'll excuse me, I'm going back to my office."*

We have to give Michelle a great deal of credit for "ruling over her spirit." Many women (and men) in a similar situation would have reacted with rage, insults, or maybe even the delivery of a smack in the face! Michelle resisted these understandable urges, and managed to keep her cool. At the same time, she was not passive or subservient to Mr. Forbes: she calmly and politely but *assertively* made her displeasure known to the boss.

In the Judaic tradition, anger is closely allied with *pride* or *arrogance*. As Rabbis Byron L. Sherwin and Seymour J. Cohen put it, "Anger places the ego at the center, displacing God and others, and causing the alienation of relationships." Sherwin and Cohen add, astutely, that "the paradox of anger is that while focusing on the ego, it causes one to lose control of the self" (Sherwin and Cohen 2001, 84). We'll say much more about pride and arrogance in Chapter 6.

On the other hand, we can learn a great deal about a person when he or she is angry. As a famous 15th century code of Jewish ethics puts it, "When one is angry, one's true nature can be recognized" (from *Orhot Zaddikim*, cited in Sherwin and Cohen 2001, 84). The true mensch is not necessarily a person who never gets angry—essentially the nature of a god or an automaton!—but rather, one who knows how to *express and channel anger in a constructive manner, in order to correct some injustice*. Indeed, as Sherwin and Cohen point out, "*Orhot Zaddikim* also discusses a positive side to anger; i.e., anger is a necessary spur to survival, and…a necessary stimulus in confronting evil and evil people" (Sherwin and Cohen 2001, 252).

For example, Michelle might consider meeting with the other female partners of her firm, and organizing some kind of support group or committee to look into the issue of sexual harassment. Or, if Michelle wanted to confront Mr. Forbes's boorish behavior more directly, she and her colleagues might arrange a meeting with him, in which they present their grievances as a group—or even consider suing him for sexual harassment. (Clearly, the latter course carries with it substantial professional and personal risks.)

The point is simply that anger is not to be suppressed or extirpated entirely in the face of injustice or evil; rather, it should serve as a finely honed instrument to promote beneficial change. Aristotle (384–322 B.C.E.) may have anticipated some of these Judaic ideas in his *Nichomachean Ethics*, when he said, "The good-tempered [person] is always angry under the right circumstances, with the right people, in the right manner and degree, at the right time, and for the right length of time" (Aristotle 1962, Book IV, chapter 5).

Jim had come home late, after a rough day at the office. His wife, Karen, had also come home late from her nursing job at the pediatric intensive care unit. Both Jim and Karen were "stressed out" and emotionally exhausted. Neither had made any plans at all for dinner, and neither was in any mood to cook. Karen turned to Jim with a look of exasperation and snapped, "You don't get it, do you? I have to deal with sick kids all day, and then I come home to find out that I'm supposed to cook dinner! That's just plain selfish on your part! How about taking charge for once and picking up something on your way home, or even cooking us a meal, for godssake!" Jim felt hurt and angry upon hearing this diatribe from Karen, believing with some justice that he had been criticized unfairly: after all, he had not suggested that it was Karen's job to cook dinner. But Jim also understood that Karen had been dealing all day with sick and perhaps dying children; that her job placed enormous demands upon her; and that she was entitled to "lose it a little" upon returning home and finding that neither of them had thought about dinner. Jim turned to Karen and said, "Hon, you're right. I could have picked up something for us. I'm sorry, I just didn't think of it. I know we've both had a rough day. How about if we just order a pizza now, or I can whip us up some eggs?"

A mensch not only controls his own anger, but also knows how to *absorb or deflect anger expressed by others*. In Proverbs (15:1), we are told, "A soft answer turns away anger." As Rabbi Lori Forman advises, "The next time you come up against anger, see if you can respond with a soft or gentle word to disarm its acceleration" (Olitzky and Forman 1999, 26). I think the Rabbis would conclude that, in this instance, Jim had responded like a mensch!

Incidentally, a recent study led by Dr. Jean-Philippe Gouin appearing in the December 19, 2007, issue of *Brain, Behavior and Immunity* found that healing of skin blisters (an index of immune system health) occurred more quickly in those who expressed anger calmly than in those who "flew off the handle." As the BBC reported, "Whether one directed one's anger externally or internally proved to have no bearing on recovery—what was crucial was just how much control the individual was able to exert over their feelings."

Perhaps the Rabbis of the Talmudic era were ahead of our modern-day scientists?

PERSONAL ENCOUNTER:
HOW HILLEL RESTRAINED HIS ANGER

Hillel the Elder, who lived in the first century B.C.E., was one of the greatest of the great Talmudic sages. He is perhaps best known for two teachings: "If

I am not for myself, who is for me? When I am for myself only, what am I? And if not now, when?" (Pirke Avot 1:14); and that famous formulation of the "Golden Rule," "Do not do unto others what you would not have them do unto you" (Shabbat 31a*)*. There is a wonderful story in the Talmud concerning Hillel's renowned powers of self-control in the face of provocation. We find Hillel the victim of a perverse wager: two men bet four hundred *zuz* (a large sum!) on whether either one of them can make Hillel angry. One of the men presents himself at Hillel's home over and over again, asking what most of us would term ridiculous questions—for example, "Why are the heads of Babylonians round?" and "Why are the eyes of the Palmyreans bleariest?" Yet, time after time, Hillel does not berate the man or disparage his questions; instead, Hillel responds in each case, "My son, you have asked a great question!" Finally, the provocateur gives up. He tells Hillel, in effect, "I hope there aren't many more of you in Israel, because I just lost four hundred zuz on account of you!" Hillel replies, "Always be careful and watch your temper. It is worth that you should lose four hundred zuz because of Hillel, and even another four hundred zuz; but no matter what you do, Hillel will not lose his temper" (Shabbat 31a; in ibn Chaviv 1999, 80).

Mitch had spent four years in his PhD program, and was "ABD" in the field of English Literature: "All But Dissertation." Unfortunately, Mitch was having constant disagreements with his dissertation supervisor. The supervisor kept insisting on changes in Mitch's arguments, but no matter what Mitch did, his supervisor never seemed to be satisfied. This was taking a toll on both Mitch and his fiancée, who complained that Mitch was "falling apart under the pressure." Mitch began to drink increasing amounts of wine, and would find excuse after excuse for avoiding work on his thesis. When his fiancée confronted Mitch on these behaviors, he replied, "I just don't have time to get the work done. There are too many distractions. And besides, no matter what I do, this clown is never satisfied!" Mitch began to sleep in until late in the afternoon, and spent more and more time wandering around a near-by shopping mall. His explanation was, "There's a bookstore I go to just to clear my head. It's important that I approach my work feeling refreshed."

Many of us who have experienced pressure and frustration in an academic or business setting will sympathize with Mitch—who wouldn't be driven to distraction, given a supervisor who is always criticizing, and a task that seems insurmountable? Yet the Talmud tells us that a real mensch must find the self-discipline and "stick-to-itiveness" to get back to work.

At the beginning of this chapter, we quoted Rabbi Tarfon to the effect that, "The day is short, the task is great, the workers are lazy, and reward is great, and the Master of the house is insistent" (Pirke Avot 2:20). What did Rabbi Tarfon mean by that? God, of course, is the "Master" for whom we are—or should be!—working. But as human beings, we tend to get lazy, despite the potential rewards that come from spiritual growth. Especially when faced with a complex or frustrating task, we tend to react like Mitch: we avoid, we rationalize, and we find a multitude of unhealthy distractions. This is not the way of the mensch, of course!

The foundational text for the teaching of Pirke Avot 2:20 may be found in Proverbs 6:6–11: "Go to the ant, O sluggard; consider her ways, and be wise. Without having any chief, officer or ruler, she prepares her food in summer, and gathers her sustenance in harvest. How long will you lie there, O sluggard? When will you arise from your sleep?"

Lieber notes that "one should not waste a moment of the precious few years…granted in this world. Life is a fleeting opportunity to gather treasure; once the time is up… [we] can no longer earn anything" (Lieber 1995, 124). On the other hand, if we are good stewards of our time, we will find ways to gather spiritual treasure. As Toperoff remarks, "if we divided our days into well defined compartments, we should find ample time to satisfy all our needs, material and spiritual" (Toperoff 1997, 130).

The role of study in the Judaic tradition can hardly be stressed enough. The Talmud tells us that, "in the hour when an individual is brought before the heavenly court for judgment…", one of the questions the person is asked is, "Did you set aside regular time for Torah study?" (Babylonian Talmud, Shabbat 31a; in Telushkin 1994, 3). On the other hand, the Rabbis did not intend us *only* to study. They knew that we must earn a living, and encouraged the acquisition of some practical skill. The mensch must strike a balance between the active and the contemplative life. Thus, in Pirke Avot (2:2), Rabban Gamliel tells us: "The study of Torah combined with an occupation is an excellent thing, for the exertion demanded by both together causes sin to be forgotten, while any Torah study without work ultimately fails and causes sin."

The lesson for the *mensch* is to avoid becoming what in Yiddish is known as a *luftmensch*. This is usually defined as "an impractical contemplative person having no definite business or income" (dictionary.com). (The reader will recall our description of Morty, the *schnorrer!*). The term *luftmensch* also carries the connotation of someone who is impractical, quixotic, or "spacey." In contrast, the idea of self-discipline in Judaism entails productive labor.

Furthermore, study without *ethical action* is not praised by the Rabbis. As Borowitz and Schwartz make clear, "Torah is doing." Indeed, "a man who has no good deeds to his credit, though he has studied Torah, is like one who builds a structure and lays down a foundation of clay bricks and puts the stones above that. Then even a little water will undermine the building" (Elisha ben Abuyah in Avot de Rabbi Natan, 24; in Borowitz and Schwartz

1999, 257–8). In essence, if we do not transform study of Torah into practice of its commandments, our spiritual "home" will ultimately be washed away. We will have much more to say about study and the mensch's responsibility to acquire wisdom in Chapter 18, Acquiring Knowledge and Wisdom.

PERSONAL ENCOUNTER: MOSHE BEN MAIMON (MAIMONIDES) AND THE IDEA OF SELF-DISCIPLINE

Maimonides (1135–1204) must have been one of the most self-disciplined individuals in the history of Judaic scholarship. Imagine spending your adult life fleeing persecution in your native country; working as a physician in an alien culture; dealing with the death of your beloved sibling while supporting your family; and all the while producing the most voluminous and influential corpus of Jewish philosophy in all of the Middle Ages! As the great Maimonides scholar Isadore Twersky put it, "Maimonides' life was a mosaic of anxiety, tribulation, and, at best, incredibly strenuous work and intellectual exertion" (Twersky 1972, 1).

Maimonides understood self-discipline primarily as a "cognitive-behavioral" skill. Indeed, in many ways, Maimonides was the "father" of our modern field of cognitive-behavioral therapy or CBT (Pies 1997). Here is what Maimonides has to say about self-discipline:

> The more mental training man has, the less affected he will be by luck or misfortune. He will not get excited over a very fortunate event and will not exaggerate its value. Likewise, if one meets disaster, he will not be disturbed and aggrieved, but will bear it valiantly (Minkin, 1987, 389).

Furthermore, according to Maimonides, we acquire healthy, balanced dispositions or character traits only by *constant practice* of "the middle way":

> Let him practice again and again the actions prompted by those dispositions which are the mean between the extremes and repeat them continually until they become easy and...no longer irksome...whoever walks in this way secures for himself happiness and blessing (Kranzler, 1993, 54).

At times, Maimonides can seem unduly "stoical" or even unfeeling in his austere beliefs. Yet I believe that much of his philosophy of self-control developed in reaction to the death of his beloved brother, David, who was lost at sea. It was a blow from which Maimonides may never have recovered fully—but his philosophy of self-mastery is still well worth emulating. We will say much more about moderation and "the middle way" in Chapter 5.

Chapter Five

Moderation and "The Middle Way"

Moderation and "The Middle Way"
Be not over-righteous...

—Ecclesiastes 7:16

In the future world, a man will have to give an accounting for every good thing his eyes saw, but of which he did not eat.

—Yerushalm, Kiddushin 4:12 (66d); cited in Telushkin 2000, 96

Eat a third and drink a third and leave the remaining third of your stomach empty. Then, when you get angry, there will be sufficient room for your rage.

—Babylonian Talmud, Gittin 70a; quoted in Klagsbrun 1980, 219

[The individual] should not prohibit for himself, by vows and oaths, things that are permitted.

—Maimonides, Laws Concerning Character Traits 3:1; cited in Weiss and Butterworth 1983, 34

Fundamentally, Judaism is a religion of moderation. The mensch is neither monk nor libertine—but rather, a man or woman who wisely and happily takes "the middle path." To be sure: we do find occasional exhortations in Judaism that speak to the merits of the ascetic life; for example, "The Torah was given in the desert, teaching us that to merit Torah, a man must renounce himself like the desert" (Pesikta de-Rab Kahana; quoted in Baron 1997). But in general, Judaism frowns on the extreme measures called for by such austere philosophies. On the contrary, as Bokser puts it, "God created man

26

and placed him into this world to enjoy the bounty of nature that is produced through the creative labor of human beings" (Bokser 1989, 22). Maimonides (quoted above) is particularly clear on the moral bankruptcy of extreme self-denial:

> Perhaps a man will say, "Since desire, honor, and the like constitute a bad way and remove a man from the world, I shall completely separate myself from them and go to the other extreme." So he does not eat meat, nor drink wine, nor take a wife, nor live in a decent dwelling, nor wear decent clothing…This, too, is a bad way and it is forbidden to follow it (*Laws Concerning Character Traits 3:1*; cited in Weiss and Butterworth 1983, 34).

It is clear, finally, that our earlier discussion of "self-mastery and self-discipline" shades almost imperceptibly into our present topic of *moderation*; for it usually requires self-mastery to avoid the Scylla of self-indulgence and the Charybdis of self-abnegation.

Callie was a single woman in her late 30s, known in her circle of friends as "Crazy Callie." She lived alone and was now working in a temp job, which she described as "really, really boring." Callie described herself as a "good time girl" and liked to recall her college days and all the "great times" she had back then, "You know, partying and stuff." Callie confided to Brad, her latest boyfriend, "When I was in junior high, my favorite song was by Cyndi Lauper: 'Girls Just Wanna Have Fun'!" Callie had been through numerous relationships with men, but "None of them ever took," as she put it. "I'm usually just too wild for most of the men I meet." Callie had developed the habit of sleeping until well past one in the afternoon, usually after "partying" all night and "getting a little stoned." Sometimes, Callie would spend the entire afternoon in a wine bar or bistro, "just having a few drinks and schmoozing." She acknowledged weekly use of alcohol, marijuana, and "a little coke, just, like, now and then." Over the years, Callie had managed to hold down a series of low-paying jobs, usually only for a few months. "Then I wind up getting the axe…like, my bosses hate me 'cause I just have so much fun and they are, like, living such dull lives." Whatever money Callie had left over at the end of the month went toward "movies, videos, and clothes."

Miriam was the scourge of her household, when it came to strict observation of Jewish law. Although both she and her husband, Jeff, were "Orthodox"Jews, Miriam seemed to find religious rulings and regulations Jeff had never heard of! For example, Miriam insisted that the entire family use a separate set of drinking glasses for "meat" or "milk" meals, even though their rabbi had told Jeff this was not required by Orthodox Jewish law (Kolatch 2000, 314).

Similarly, Miriam insisted that at least eight hours pass before anyone in the family who had consumed meat could eat dairy products. When little Rivka, who was six years old, violated this rule, Miriam scolded her and gave her a light "swat" on the backside. Again, their rabbi had told both Jeff and Miriam that the eight hour waiting period was "more than even the most stringent dietary law requires" (Kolatch, 2000, 316). To Jeff's great embarrassment, Miriam had actually replied to the rabbi, "Rabbi Cohen, with all due respect: surely you must know that fatty meat residue clings to the palate and the teeth for at least eight hours!" In recent years, Jeff and Miriam had also had some sexual tensions in their marriage. Miriam insisted, for example, on eight "clean days" after her menstrual period ended. Orthodox Jewish law requires abstinence from sex during a woman's menstrual period; however, this is ordinarily extended to seven days after the woman's flow of blood has ceased (Kolatch, 2000, 145). Miriam insisted on the "extra day," just in case "I might not have noticed a little bleeding." When Jeff would gently chide Miriam for "waiting so long," she would respond testily, saying, "You men should learn to have some patience!"

Callie and Miriam may seem, at first glance, like "complete opposites"—Callie, the party girl; and Miriam, the ultra-ultra-Orthodox matron. But from the standpoint of most rabbinical teachings, Callie and Miriam are really cut from the same psychological cloth: each has gone to an extreme in her approach to life. (By the way, I could easily have created two very similar vignettes, using two *men* as examples—extremism as a life-style knows no "gender" boundaries!) To appreciate the nature of Callie's departure from rabbinical teaching, we turn to Pirke Avot, 3:14: "Rabbi Dosa the son of Harkinas says: Morning sleep, midday wine, children's talk, and sitting in the assembly houses of the ignorant drive a person out of the world."

It is important to understand that the Rabbis of the Talmud were not opposed to enjoying life, in moderation—far from it! But Callie has gone well beyond enjoying the pleasures of life in moderation. Indeed, her dependence on alcohol ("midday wine") and other drugs is not only a sign of immoderate substance use, but also a desecration of her body. As Telushkin points out, "Jewish law prohibits one from engaging in self-destructive behavior" (Telushkin 2000, 115). This ordinarily includes the use of powerful and destructive substances, such as nicotine, marijuana, and cocaine. (Although there is nothing in the Talmud to prohibit tobacco use, most modern rabbinical teaching has inclined toward the prohibition of smoking. See Telushkin 2000, 51–54). Moreover, Callie's "partying" has a nearly compulsive quality to it. Her afternoons spent in wine bars and bistros (from a rabbinical perspective, "the assembly houses of the ignorant") signify an immoderate focus on pleasure—and, one suspects, an attempt to "numb" some kind of psychic pain or emptiness.

> ...sleep here is a metaphor for excessive relaxation. In moderation, respite is necessary to preserve one's health, and in fact one should be careful to relax after any strenuous activity...enjoyed in moderation, the pleasures of life enable a person to maintain his emotional stability as well as a healthy sense of joie de vivre (Lieber, 1995, 165).

All this notwithstanding, the moderate consumption of food and alcohol is not condemned in rabbinical Judaism. Wine, of course, has a special place in Jewish law, since, on Shabbat (Sabbath), "the Kiddush prayer is twice recited over wine; and at the Passover seder, four cups of wine are consumed" (Telushkin 2000, 285). Food is to be enjoyed in moderation, as well. Indeed, Telushkin tells us that Rabbi Elazar would set aside money "so that he could eat every kind of food at least once a year" (Telushkin 2000, 96).

Drunkenness, as a rule, is severely condemned in Talmudic teachings. Thus, we are told that one who is really drunk "is not allowed to pray, and if he does, his prayer is an abomination" (Eruvin 64a; in ibn Chaviv, 150). And yet—in what may seem like remarkable laxity in a religion!—highly circumscribed intoxication is not utterly prohibited in Judaism. In fact, on the joyous holiday of Purim, outright drunkenness is considered a commandment! Thus, "A person should become so drunk on Purim that he cannot tell the difference between 'Cursed be Haman,' and 'Blessed be Mordechai'" (Babylonian Talmud, Megillah 7b; cited in Telushkin 1994, 231).

As Telushkin notes, this degree of drunkenness—in which one doesn't know the difference between the villain, Haman, and the hero, Mordechai—represents "the deepest level of drunkenness imaginable" (Telushkin 1994, 231). Of course, the Rabbis undoubtedly envisioned such drunkenness on Purim as occurring in the bosom of a loving and "care-taking" family—one that could ensure the safety of a drunken family member. This clearly cannot be guaranteed when one is drinking in some dismal bar, as was the case with poor Callie. Moreover, some have interpreted the commandment to apply only to men, and only to the daytime meal. The Rama (Rabbi Moshe Isserles, ca. 1530–1572) taught that one could fulfill this mitzvah simply by drinking a bit more than usual and then taking a nap (Weinbach 2010)!

And now, what about Miriam? On one level, we might admire Miriam for her fierce—if not fanatical—dedication to Jewish law and ritual. But on another level, Miriam is really the "inverted image" of Callie. Instead of excessive dedication to sensual pleasure, Miriam has become excessively focused on the minutiae of religious observance, *beyond what is actually prohibited by the Torah*. Maimonides instructs us,

Therefore the wise men commanded that a man only abstain from things forbidden by the Torah alone. He shall not prohibit for himself, by vows and oaths, things that are permitted....Those who fast continually are in this class [of excessive practitioners]; they do not follow the good way (*Laws Concerning Character Traits* 3:1; cited in Weiss and Butterworth 1983, 34).

Following the teachings of Aristotle (in his *Nichomachean Ethics*), Maimonides advocated the "middle way" in nearly all our thoughts, behaviors, and appetites. He tells us that,

Good actions are those balanced in the mean between two extremes, both of which are bad; one of them is an excess and the other a deficiency...Lust is the first extreme and total insensibility to pleasure the other extreme; both of them are completely bad...in like manner, liberality is the mean between miserliness and extravagance; courage is the mean between rashness and cowardice; wit is the mean between buffoonery and dullness; humility is the mean between haughtiness and abasement; generosity is the mean between prodigality and stinginess (Maimonides, *Eight Chapters*, chapter 4; cited in Weiss and Butterworth 1983, 67).

In short, the mensch tries to avoid extremes in nearly all areas of emotional, interpersonal, and spiritual life. One important exception to this principle is in the realm of *humility*. Here, we are often admonished by the Rabbis to emulate Moses, who was described in the Torah (Numbers 12:3) as "*exceedingly* humble, more than any other man on the face of the earth." We will have much more to say on "Humility and Simplicity" (humbly, we hope!) in Chapter 6.

One other point regarding Miriam's excessive religiosity: it has clearly disrupted the emotional and interpersonal lives of her family, as excesses of any kind usually do. To digress just a bit, we should mention the important concept of *shalom bayit*—the "peace of the household," so valued in the rabbinical literature. When we consider Miriam's scolding and swatting her daughter, we can appreciate the destructive effects of excessive piety, or of any extreme position that leads to family strife. As Shelly Kapnek Rosenberg puts it in her instructive book, *Raising a Mensch*,

Our children's earliest learning environment—their *bayit* (home)—is the first place they learn about and experience peaceful behavior...to teach our children peace, we must work to control our own tempers...we must be especially careful never to strike out—physically or verbally—at our children. When we are angry, we must try to find a way to move past it and to work together with our children to find an answer to the problem (Rosenberg 2003, 85).

*Morris was in his mid-60s when Betty, his beloved wife of 40 years, died of a ruptured brain aneurysm. Because her death was both unexpected and nearly instantaneous, Morris was thrown into a state of shock. For several weeks, he barely spoke to anybody, even to those who came to comfort him. He hardly ate any solid food for the first month after Betty's death, getting by on juice and the occasional bowl of soup. After his sister, Faye, recommended that Morris speak with a "grief counselor," he appeared to improve for a few weeks, returning to his usual social and eating patterns. Morris had never considered himself a religious individual. His father was Jewish, his mother Episcopalian, and the family had never been inculcated in the ways of any particular faith. "We were raised as agnostics and independent thinkers," Morris's sister observed, adding, "Politics was always much more important in our home than religion." However, in the wake of his wife's death, Morris began to pour through the mourning rituals of several religious traditions. From the Jewish tradition, Morris imbibed the idea of reciting the mourner's Kaddish, a prayer whose central intent is the magnification and sanctification of God's name. But whereas Jewish law requires that the Kaddish be recited only in the presence of a minyan (a quorum of ten—see Kolatch 2000, 198), Morris began reciting the prayer three or four times a day, while alone at home. He also shaved his head, and started wearing the same clothing day after day, for several weeks (Jewish law would permit neither of these behaviors). Having read that in the Hindu tradition, mourners cover all religious pictures in the house (Beliefnet, n.d.), Morris put pillow cases over all the artwork in his house, which was quite extensive. He had already covered mirrors in the house, as is customary for the seven days of mourning (*shiva*) in the Jewish tradition, but Morris kept the mirrors covered for several months after Betty's death. Finally, Morris decided to take a six-month sabbatical from his teaching position at a local community college, "so that I can properly honor Betty's memory."*

Mourning, as most psychotherapists know, is a highly individualized process. It is said that Queen Victoria mourned for her deceased husband, Prince Albert, for more than forty years—even ordering her servants to lay out her late husband's clothes each morning (Horrall 2004). While we must never pressure the bereaved person to, "Get over it already!"—a common impulse among well meaning family and friends—we also need to recognize that *healthy* mourning typically does have some limits. Indeed, the Rabbis were very clear that mourning—like nearly everything else in life—ought to be guided by the principle of moderation.

After the destruction of the Second Temple in the year 70 C.E./A.D, many Jews became extremely ascetic, to demonstrate their sense of loss. For example, they refrained from eating meat or drinking wine, which they associated with luxury and joyful living. The Rabbis of that era were not pleased with this development. "*We should not mourn excessively,*" they said, "because we must not impose upon the community a hardship that would be difficult to bear" (Bava Batra 60b; quoted in Kolatch 2000, 192, italics added).

Similarly, Maimonides sought to limit the duration and even the nature of the mourning process. Thus, in his *Mishneh Torah* (Hilkhot Avel 13:1), Maimonides advises "three days for weeping, seven days for lamenting, and thirty days for [abstaining] from cutting the hair" (cited in Halkin and Hartman 1985, 291). More strikingly, Maimonides prescribed a well defined behavioral procedure for "weaning" the mourner from the grieving process:

> During the first three days, the mourner should think of himself as if a sword is resting upon his neck; from the third to the seventh day as if it is lying in the corner; thereafter, as if it is moving toward him in the street. Reflections of this nature will put him on his mettle, he will bestir himself... (Hilkhot Avel 13:12; in Halkin and Hartman 1985, 292).

In essence, this is a form of "guided imagery"—quite like the methods used in the treatment of various phobic and post-traumatic disorders (Pies 1997, 28).

What do these attempts to circumscribe mourning have to do with being a mensch? Fundamentally, in my view, they epitomize the need for *preserving our emotional equilibrium,* so that others can count on us. A mensch, after all, is someone to be relied upon, in good times and bad. A mensch cannot be a "rock of Gibraltar" for others if he or she is laid low by self-imposed and *unlimited* mourning. Put another way, beyond a certain point—which, to be sure, will differ from person to person—*excessive* mourning may unintentionally become a form of self-indulgence. I do not mean to condemn those who choose to mourn for periods longer than traditionally sanctioned by society. Nor do I, as a psychiatrist, mean to suggest that bereaved persons who become clinically depressed can simply "turn off" their emotions like a water spout. I am simply saying that a mensch is someone who *strives to move beyond unbounded sorrow*, in so far as he or she is ready and able.

On the other hand, a frivolous or callous *indifference* to the loss of a loved one is certainly *not* a quality of the mensch. As Telushkin reminds us, with respect to the death of a parent,

> the refusal to mourn a parent's death for seven days is a gross form of disrespect. To carry on with one's life as if nothing significant has happened is essentially to declare the deceased's life and death to be insignificant (Telushkin 2000, 448).

In short, the mensch strives to find "the middle way" between unbounded grief and unfeeling indifference.

PERSONAL ENCOUNTER: "MODERATION" FROM A MODERN MASTER

Rabbi Berel Wein has been a congregational rabbi, a yeshiva dean, a prolific author, and a lecturer throughout the world. His comments on the final chapter of Pirke Avot are well worth reading, as they speak to us of ancient truths, but in a modern idiom. Chapter 6 is not a part of Pirke Avot per se; rather, it is a collection of supplementary teachings (*baraitot*), probably added in the fourth or fifth century C.E. Chapter 6 is known as *Perek Kinyan Torah*, or *Chapter of the Acquisition of Torah*, since it is almost entirely devoted to praise of Torah knowledge and study (Wein 2003, 230). The portion that concerns us is Mishnah 6, which speaks to the *48 traits required for acquiring Torah*. Among these is "moderation" in six critical areas. In Rabbi Wein's translation (Wein 2003, 252–3), the areas are: *limited business activity; limited sexual activity; limited pleasure; limited sleep; limited conversation;* and *limited laughter.* What does it mean to set "limits" in each of these areas? Rabbi Wein provides us with some guidelines for our own age:

> The Torah advocates moderation. There are certain areas and pursuits in life that, if not contained and regulated, easily become all consuming. The pursuit of commerce and wealth certainly is addictive if it is not balanced by the perspective of family and Torah living. One must earn a living, but that requirement must be balanced with other equally important facets of life. Torah knowledge and its attendant benefits cannot be acquired unless one is willing to minimize the drive to pursue wealth at all costs…The counsel of moderation also extends to pleasures, leisure, even civic activity and studies of the world… Pleasure and enjoyment are necessary ingredients of life, but they can lead to obsessive behavior…Time, too, must be managed. We all need sleep, but most people can probably do very well with less sleep than they think they need… Careful conversation and measured speech are requirements for Torah living… Say little and do much is a maxim of traditional Judaism. Conversation for the sake of conversation is an addictive form of behavior, especially in our world of constant noise and sound, of talk-shows and incessant 24–hour a day news networks…Humor is one of the great human defense mechanisms, and Jews are famous for their ability to inject humor into life…but there is a great difference between humor and…a general attitude of not taking matters seriously. Such attitudes often lead to cynicism and mockery of others (Wein 2003, 252–3).

Chapter Six

Humility and Flexibility

Rabbi Levitas of Yavneh said: Be of an exceedingly humble spirit, for the hope of the human being is decay.

—Pirke Avot 4:4

Rabbi Yochanan said in the name of Rabbi Shimon bar Yochai: A person who is conceited is as though he worships idols.

—Sotah 4b; in ibn Chaviv 1999, 438

A person should always be gentle and flexible like a reed [in his relationships with others] and never hard and unyielding like a cedar tree.

—Taanit 20b; in ibn Chaviv 1999, 303

Whoever seeks greatness, greatness runs away from him; and whoever runs away from greatness, greatness pursues him.

—Eruvin 13b; in ibn Chaviv 1999, 138

If you make yourself small in your in your own eyes, you will be big in the eyes of others and of [God]. This is a true test of humility.

—Sefer Orchos Tzadikim, Sha'ar Ha'Anova; in Forsythe 2008

It is impossible to resist beginning this chapter with an anecdote from Rabbi Joseph Telushkin, in his wonderful work, *The Book of Jewish Values*. He relates how the famous architect, Frank Lloyd Wright, once served as a witness in a court case and identified himself as "The greatest living architect." Later, when he was chastised by his wife for such arrogance, Wright is said to have replied, "I had no choice. I was under oath" (Telushkin 2000, 104).

Few of us (including this writer) can escape the charge of immodesty at some time in our lives—though we may sometimes wrap our pride in the garb of self-effacement. Nonetheless, the rabbinical tradition counts humility (in Hebrew, *anava*) as one of the foundational virtues of the mensch. Conversely, pride is seen as one of the greatest sins—comparable to idol worship! As Rabbi Jeff Forsythe has succinctly put it, *anava* is "the foundation for all good character and behavior. Intellect must be preceded by fear of sin, which must be preceded by humility, which is the root of all good. Nothing good, true, right or lasting can be achieved without *anava*" (Forsythe 2008).

Genuine humility, I would suggest, is recognized less by what a person *thinks* than by how he or she *actually behaves when dealing with the wishes and views of others.* In this sense, the virtue of humility is bound up with the character traits of *flexibility, tact, and respect for others' feelings.* Thus, when we are taught that *"A person should always be gentle and flexible like a reed,"* we are being led toward a kind of *interpersonal behavior.* Indeed, in the Talmud (Taanit 20b), the anecdote used to illustrate the point about the reed involves a very specific incident involving Rabbi Elazar, son of Rabbi Shimon. It seems that R. Elazar was feeling quite pleased with himself, having just mastered some Torah lessons with his teacher. On his way home, R. Elazar happens upon a "very ugly person" whom he then gratuitously insults! Eventually, R. Elazar asks forgiveness of the poor man, and the latter grants it, provided that R. Elazar "should not get into the habit [of insulting people]" (ibn Chaviv 1999, 303). The Talmudic interpretation is that R. Elazar was in a "self-admiring frame of mind that prompted the disparaging remark" (Maharsha; cited in ibn Chaviv 1999, 303).

The Talmud also leaves us with the clear teaching that, in the long run, it is the gentle and flexible reed that survives the storm—for it is sustained by many roots, and bends in the gale. The "hard and unyielding" cedar may be tall and impressive, but it is easily uprooted in a stiff wind (see Forsythe 2008, and Taanit 20a-20b). And so, ironically, it is humility that is self-preserving; and arrogance, self-defeating.

Karl was the CEO of one of the busiest and most successful companies in New York, a computer software firm that Karl had "built with my own hands" from a modest beginning in his own home, more than a decade ago. But Karl's success was a function of many lucky breaks, and more than a handful of supportive friends, advisers, and patrons. One day, Karl's friend and junior partner, Burt, knocked on Karl's door, announcing, "I need to talk to you about a decision I've made." Burt had always been "like a son" to Karl, and Burt considered Karl "a mentor—really, more like an older brother or even a father." To Karl's shock and amazement, Burt announced that he was leaving the company to start his own software firm—one that would be competing directly with Karl's company. Karl felt angry and betrayed. The thought that kept going through his mind, even as Burt spoke, was "How dare you do this to me? I practically raised you, you treacherous little ingrate!" But as Burt continued to talk, outlining his plans and actually asking for Karl's help, a scene from long ago came to mind. Karl saw himself sitting with his own father, breaking the news to him that he, Karl, would not be going into the family furniture business as his father had long hoped. Rather than react with anger, his father had heard Karl out, and responded gently and with understanding. Summoning this memory, Karl said to Burt, "Well, Burt, I'll miss you here. And I guess it will be a little strange, competing with you. But I understand that you want to strike out on your own. Who knows? Maybe we'll find some opportunities to collaborate on some new software ideas!"

Karl showed himself to be a mensch, in several respects. Although our present concern is with "humility," we can say that Karl exhibited virtually all the characteristics of the mensch we have discussed thus far:

• Kindness and Compassion
• Generosity and Charity
• Self-mastery and Self-discipline
• Moderation and "The Middle Way"
• Humility and Flexibility

Clearly, there is no sharp boundary between any one of these character traits and any of the others; in a sense, they are all neighboring colors in a single spectrum of virtue. But perhaps one could argue, as Rabbi Forsythe suggests above, that humility is the *foundation* of nearly all these other virtues. In effect, one begins with the question, "What am I? Am I so high and mighty a being that I have all the answers? Am I so god-like that I deserve all the world's honor and respect? Or—if not—am I just a fallible human being, trying to make my way in this hard and troubled world? But if that is what I am, then perhaps I must find a way to deal with my fellow human beings that reflects my place in the Universe. Perhaps I can moderate my anger when provoked. Perhaps I can master my sense of outrage when I feel betrayed. Perhaps I can be generous with my love and time to those who struggle as I once did. And perhaps I can show those less fortunate than I a measure of kindness and compassion."

Although our focus is on Talmudic and rabbinical teachings, these sentiments are perhaps best summed up by the 15th century Catholic monk, Thomas a Kempis, whose lessons on humility are truly universal: "there is no man without his faults; none without his burden. None is sufficient in himself; none is wise in himself; therefore we must support one another, comfort, help, teach, and advise one another." (a Kempis 1995, 40–41).

Mr. and Mrs. Green were determined that their daughter, Susan, would have the most lavish wedding on the planet. Susan's mother, Belle, had "spared no expense" in hiring the best caterer in the city and renting the poshest hotel for the reception. Even the band had been flown in from New York at great expense. Susan herself was ambivalent regarding her parents' plans and had actually expressed a preference for a smaller and more intimate wedding, which was also the preference of her fiancé, David. But Susan's parents were insistent—the wedding would be planned their way. As her mother put it, "Honey, I know it seems like a big to-do, but believe me, some-day you'll thank your father and me." When Susan protested, her mother became quite angry, saying, "Don't be a little fool! This is your one chance to get what you deserve—and to give your parents what we deserve!" Susan was momentarily stunned. Although she was angry, she paused to reflect on her mother's life, and how, as a young woman, Belle desperately wanted to become a nurse. Her own parents had thwarted this ambition, arguing that Belle should "settle down with a good man." Rather than return her mother's anger with her own, Susan said, "Mom, I disagree with you, but I'll try to respect your wishes."

In this rather sad vignette, we find that humility has eluded Susan's parents on several levels. First, there is the obvious issue of the lavish wedding—something Susan's mother was far more invested in than Susan. In the Judaic tradition, we find the term *tzeniut,* usually translated as "modesty." A reasonable definition of *tzeniut* is "the norms of modest behavior, attitude, and dress prescribed by the Torah" (Ginsburgh 2008). There has been much controversy, in the feminist and post-feminist literature, regarding the application of the term *tzeniut* to women and their appearance. As Borowitz and Schwartz rightly note, "the Talmud was a product of its times, echoing the other male-dominated cultures of the Middle East…[hence]…How women stand, how they walk, what they show of themselves, and what they keep concealed are all part of the tireless rabbinic policing of proper female behavior" (Borowitz and Schwartz 1999, 156–7). Let us stipulate, then, that some rabbinical texts may apply the term *tzeniut* in what nowadays might be termed a "sexist" manner.

Nonetheless, we can probe for a deeper and more universal sense of the term *tzeniut,* and apply it to the attitude of Susan's parents. We begin with the observation of the medieval philosopher-poet Solomon ibn Gabirol (ca. 1021–1058 C.E.) that "Modesty is meekness and wisdom combined" (Mivhar Hapeninim; cited in Borowitz and Schwartz 1999, 150). Thus, the modest person—and the mensch—is not ostentatious, pretentious, or demanding. Moreover, the modest individual exercises *reason and discretion* in choosing how to behave. This surely includes taking into account the feelings and wishes of others. On both accounts, Susan's parents (especially her mother) were found wanting. Belle's fixation on having a big, showy wedding represents not only a lapse in "modesty," but also an insensitivity to her daughter's needs. Indeed, even after Susan's protestations, her mother responded with what the Rabbis call *azzut*—obduracy, or "hard-heartedness." This attitude is akin to the rigidity of the cedar, and is the precisely the opposite of humility and flexibility (Feldman 1999, 181). Psychologically, we may partly *account* for Belle's behavior, in light of her own thwarted ambitions: her need for a lavish wedding seems, on some level, a kind of vicarious compensation for the loss of her own dream. But this does not *excuse* Belle's behavior. In contrast, Susan's respectful and humble response in the face of her mother's provocation is a fine example of *tzeniut*: "meekness and wisdom combined."

Ben was a recently retired lawyer and entrepreneur, and an active member of his business community. When his local Chamber of Commerce approached him with an offer, Ben was very excited. The President of the local chapter, Joe, needed someone to serve as a spokesman for the city on several trips abroad—including stopovers in France, Italy, and China. Not only would the position be good for Ben's community, it would also raise funds for a local charity that Ben strongly supported. According to the job description, the spokesperson would need to be "Someone with excellent interpersonal skills, speaking ability, and negotiating prowess." Ben knew he was more than qualified for the job—after all, he was a frequent guest speaker at small business conferences, and he had negotiated several major legal transactions on behalf of the city. In truth, Ben believed he was far better qualified to take the job than anybody he knew. But Ben didn't feel it was "dignified" to "toot my own horn." He also wondered if the job might just be too much work. When Joe asked him if he would tackle the job, Ben replied, "Honestly, Joe, I don't think I have the credentials. I'm just not a great negotiator." Ben fully expected the President to protest such a "humble" declaration, and try to "talk him in" to taking the job. But instead, Joe seemed mildly annoyed, replying, "Well, if you're not interested, Ben, I guess we'll just have to find somebody else." Ben was taken aback by this rebuff, and said nothing. Ultimately, Joe offered the job to another attorney who jumped at the opportunity.

What should we make of Ben's "humble" protestation that he was not up to the job? Is this sort of attitude appropriate for the mensch? The Jewish sages recognized that humility could sometimes be carried too far—and even be transformed into a kind of vanity. Such "false humility" was discouraged by the Rabbis of the Talmud. As Sherwin and Cohen (2001, 85) put it,

> Humility is meant to be a strength, not a weakness. When a person claims humility as an excuse for inaction, it becomes a weakness rather than a strength ... such a person is abusing the virtue of humility rather than practicing it ... authentic humility may be a conduit to great accomplishments but it can never become an excuse for evading the challenges that face us.

Elaborating on this theme, Sherwin and Cohen cite the views of the Italian Jewish rabbi, kabbalist, and philosopher, Moses Hayyim Luzzatto (1707–1746): "For Luzzatto, false humility is as detestable as brazen arrogance. The individual who flaunts his humility, who is outwardly humble while inwardly proud, is one who 'takes pride in his humility' " (Sherwin and Cohen 2001, 85).

Ben's seeming humility was really an unappetizing farrago of *arrogance* ("Ben believed he was far better qualified to take the job than anybody he knew"), *laziness* ("He also wondered if the job might just be too much work"), and a perverse kind of *pride* (Ben "fully expected the President to ... 'talk him in' to taking the job").

As with so many other character traits, the Rabbis believed that the "middle path" was usually best, when it came to humility. They envisioned a kind of *dialectic* that would enable the individual to avoid the twin pitfalls of arrogance and self-abnegation. The Hasidic master, Rabbi Bunam of Przysucha, advised that

> Each person should have two pockets. In each pocket he or she should carry a slip of paper on which is written one of these two citations .... If one becomes too haughty and proud, one should ... [pull out the slip that reads] ... "I am dust and ashes," and if one becomes too self-abusing and depressed, then one should extract the slip that reads, "For my sake the world was created" (cited in Sherwin and Cohen 2001, 88).

PERSONAL ENCOUNTER: HILLEL VERSUS SHAMMAI AND THE TRAIT OF HUMILITY

We encountered the great sage, Hillel the Elder, in our earlier discussion of how Hillel mastered his anger in the face of florid provocation. Given the tight linkage between *anger* and *arrogance*, it is not surprising that Hillel was also a man of great humility. As related by Rabbi Adin Steinsaltz (1997, 3–23), Hillel came from a wealthy family that was indirectly descended from the House of David. Yet Hillel himself "came to the Land of Israel not as royalty, but as a pauper" and earned his living as a woodcutter—an occupation "which enabled him to work for only half a day, leaving the other half free for study" (Steinsaltz 1997, 4). One of Hillel's great contemporaries, Shammai, habitually disagreed with the rulings of Hillel and his "school" (*Beit Hillel*). Although Shammai was a truly great sage, he was (to be charitable) not renowned for his patience and humility. Indeed, The Talmud tells us that amid the disputes between the two schools of Hillel and Shammai, a "voice issued from Heaven" announcing that the Law "is in agreement with the School of Hillel" (Eruvin 13b; cited in Telushkin 2000, 186). Why was this so? Because, we are told, the disciples of Hillel "were kindly and humble, and because they studied their own rulings and those of the School of Shammai, and *even mentioned the teachings of the School of Shammai before their own*" (Ervin 13b; cited in Telushkin 2000, 186, italics added). To this account, Telushkin (2000, 187) adds,

> The wording of the passage suggests that Shammai's followers had grown somewhat arrogant. Certain that they possessed the truth, they no longer bothered to listen to, or discuss the arguments of, their opponents. Their overbearing self-confidence led them to become morally less impressive… and probably … to become intellectually less insightful (after all, how insightful can you be if you are studying only one side of the issue?).

In our own time, we have seen how arrogance and closed-mindedness can lead to great calamity. So many people in positions of power seem to operate under the principle, "My mind is made up—don't confuse me with facts!" May we conclude by noting, humbly if possible, that such is not the way of the mensch.

Chapter Seven

Forgiveness and Apology

Sins that are between man and God, Yom Kippur atones for them; Sins that are between man and his fellow, Yom Kippur will not atone until he appeases his fellow.

—Yoma 85b; in Feldman 1999, 139–140

No one can forgive crimes committed against someone else.

—Rabbi Abraham Joshua Heschel; quoted in Telushkin 2000, 389

Raba said, "Whose sin is forgiven? The sin of him who forgives sins [committed against him- or herself]"

—Babylonian Talmud, Megillah 28a; in Telushkin 2000, 270

R. Nehunia, the Elder, was asked by what merit he deserved long life. He said: "I have never accepted gifts, and I have always forgotten the wrongs done against me."

—Megillah 28; in Newman and Spitz 1945, 131

Forgiveness—the asking and the granting of it—is of central importance in Judaic ethics. But forgiveness (mechilah) in Judaism is no mere pronouncement or individual action, such as saying, "OK, I forgive you." Genuine forgiveness is a kind of sacred dance involving the offender and the aggrieved party—and each must make the "right moves." Forgiveness is a dialectical *process*, not a unilateral word or act. And Judaism does not allow the wrongdoer to "fudge" his or her apology, by saying to the aggrieved party, "I'm sorry for anything I may have done to offend you." If the wrongdoer has a fairly clear idea of the wrong done to a friend or loved one, he or she must apologize specifically for the act or acts (Feldman, 1999, 149). Furthermore, there are some kinds of "wrongs" that even God cannot forgive. In this respect, Judaism differs from some other major faiths, in which God's powers of forgiveness are said to be absolute.

Lenny was a middle-aged businessman who had no particular religious orientation, though his family of origin was Jewish. Still, Lenny professed a belief in "a God of some sort" and did occasionally pray—for example, when a friend or loved one was very sick. Lenny had been brooding for several years over some wrongdoing that had occurred when he was in a business partnership with Sam, who now lived in another state. Lenny had "kept the books" in the small furniture store that that he and Sam had run. One year, when his own financial situation was quite bad, Lenny had cheated Sam out of a few thousand dollars. Sam had never discovered this malfeasance, and the two had parted ways on good terms when Sam and his family left the state. But Lenny's cheating ate away at him, over the years. Finally, he decided to ask God for forgiveness. For the first time in many years, Lenny went to his local synagogue, and said a "special prayer of repentance."

In the rabbinical and Talmudic framework, Lenny's method of "repentance"—even if sincere—would be considered incomplete at best; and at worst, a self-serving sham. Lenny apparently believes that he is "off the hook" for his embezzlement of Sam's funds if he simply makes things "right with God." But the Talmud tells us otherwise. As presented in the epigraph to this chapter, we are told that, "Sins that are between man and God, Yom Kippur atones for them; Sins that are between man and his fellow, Yom Kippur will not atone until he appeases his fellow" (Yoma 85b, Feldman 1999, 139–40). The issue here is not really Yom Kippur, though the approach of this most holy day does impose a kind of "deadline" for seeking forgiveness from those we have wronged. Rather, the central moral issue is that "if an offense has been committed, *forgiveness must be sought* irrespective of the time of year" (Feldman 1999, 142, italics added); and this must begin with *restitution and apology* to the aggrieved party. Anything less—even a heart-felt prayer to God—is considered insincere or ineffectual penitence on the part of the sinner. As Rabbi Daniel Feldman puts it, "Heavenly forgiveness comes only after human forgiveness" (Feldman 1999, 144).

Rabbi Joseph Telushkin provides more specific guidance in the case of someone defrauded, such as Sam:

if you have cheated another, you must first pay the person what you owe him and then beg his forgiveness...if you are not in a position to return the money, explain your circumstances to the person you defrauded, and ask him or her to bear with you as you try to pay off as much of the debt as you can. If the person has died, you should pay the money to his or her heirs (Telushkin 2000, 388).

But what if we seek forgiveness from one we have wronged, and that person *rebuffs* us? The mensch is obligated to try again. Indeed, the offender is obligated to offer apologies *three times*, but no more than that (Feldman 1999, 144). We are not expected to spend the rest of our lives begging someone for forgiveness, but we are required to make a good faith effort.

But what about the aggrieved party? In the Judaic tradition, there is a reciprocal obligation that requires this person to accept a sincere and substantive apology—at least for "ordinary" wrongs. (More on exceptions to this shortly). Indeed, the Talmud warns that one who refuses to forgive is called *akhzari*, "cruel" (Bava Kama 92a; Feldman 1999, 151). What if you are too angry to forgive the one who has wronged you? Then, as Rabbi Telushkin puts it, "you should work on yourself. Try to enter into the other person's mind and imagine why she might have acted as she did" (Telushkin 2000, 379). Professional counseling or psychotherapy, in my experience, may also help some people reach a point where they are willing to forgive—though not forget—certain kinds of wrongdoing. (In some cases, however—for example, those involving physical abuse—forgiveness may need to await the justifiable *prosecution* of the wrongdoer).

Of course, there may be some kinds of evil acts that are beyond, or nearly beyond, human forgiveness. Telushkin notes certain "egregious and relatively rare evils ... such as requests for forgiveness made by a rapist, a kidnapper, or a mugger" that may not absolutely require our forgiveness. But that does not mean that mensch shouldn't *try* to forgive, even when such heinous acts are involved. Indeed, Telushkin cites Professor Louis Newman's *Past Imperatives: Studies in the History and Theory of Jewish Ethics* that (in Telushkin's words) "no crime committed against another should be beyond forgiveness" (Telushkin 2000, 379). Perhaps we must conclude that such situations are a matter of individual conscience, and that even a mensch may choose *not* to forgive certain kinds of wrongdoing.

Mary, a 35–year-old mother of two, was beside herself with grief and rage. She had recently learned that her seven-year-old daughter, Meagan, had been molested by a female babysitter, over the past year. The little girl herself was sullen, withdrawn, and sometimes nearly catatonic. A trauma specialist diagnosed severe post-traumatic stress syndrome (PTSD) and opined that Meagan would probably "need years of therapy to get beyond this." Mary was, of course, furious with the babysitter, who offered some dubious "explanations" of her abusive behavior. It seemed, for example, that the 18–year-old high school student had been sexually abused herself by an older cousin, when she was Meagan's age. Mary was uncomfortable with her own level of anger, and sought pastoral counseling. A clergyman in a non-denominational counseling center told Mary, "You need to come to a place in your heart where you forgive this babysitter for what she did to Meagan." This seemed "like the right thing" to Mary, and after many months, she was finally able to forgive the babysitter. Meagan, however, showed only modest signs of improvement, and continued to be nearly mute at times. She eventually required an antidepressant known to ameliorate PTSD.

On one level, we can understand and even respect the clergyman's advice to Meagan. Indeed, there are many clergy and scholars in the Christian tradition who believe that all sins can and should be forgiven (see Telushkin 2000, 389). For example, it was quite striking, after the horrendous killings of five children in an Amish school house in 2006, that some Amish community leaders advocated "forgiveness" of the murderer, "turning the other cheek…and quietly accepting what comes their way as God's will" (Collins 2006).

We can admire the Amish for their courage and compassion, while disagreeing with their concept of "forgiveness." Certainly, in the Judaic tradition, the Amish community had no more right to forgive their children's murderer than did Mary the right to forgive the babysitter who molested her daughter. For in the rabbinical ethos, *we are prohibited from forgiving on someone else's behalf.* As Telushkin explains (2000, 389–91), the only one who (in principle) can forgive a murderer is the person murdered—and since that is impossible, the rest of us cannot act in the victim's stead by conferring "forgiveness" on the murderer. Telushkin quotes Rabbi Abraham Joshua Heschel on "forgiving" the Nazis for murdering six million Jews:

> No one can forgive crimes committed against someone else. It is therefore preposterous to assume that any Jew alive can grant forgiveness for the suffering of any one of the six million people who perished…even God Himself can only forgive sins committed against Himself, not against man (Telushkin 2000, 391).

Note, however, that we *may* forgive the "indirect" suffering inflicted *on us*, as a result of someone's having harmed a friend or loved one. For example, suppose you have a brother who has been extremely cruel to your parents. Naturally, witnessing such mistreatment would have been very distressing to you. Suppose, sadly, that your parents die before your brother can apologize or make restitution to them. Are you permitted to forgive your brother for his mistreatment of *your parents*? The rabbinical answer would be *no*—only your parents would be in a position (if they were alive) to forgive your brother. But, if your brother sincerely apologizes for the "indirect" suffering he caused *you*, you are entitled to forgive him to just that extent. Indeed, to grant such forgiveness is to take the part of the mensch.

Moreover, even though there are some crimes we may be unable to forgive—both emotionally and ethically—there may be ways we can "get beyond" a state of eternal bitterness toward an evildoer. Recently, CNN News reported on a father whose son had been gunned down by a gang member in Los Angeles. The father went to court and witnessed the trial of the man charged in his son's murderer. The boy's father reported to CNN that, "he can't forgive the man who allegedly killed his son. But he says his son's death has given him a new calling: to try to bridge the divide between blacks and Latinos in Los Angeles" (Finnstrom and Cary 2008).

Ten years ago, Deana and her best friend, Meg, both found themselves interested in the same young man. But their feelings toward Steve were quite different. For Meg, Steve was the "love of her life," even though he seemed lukewarm to her overtures. For Deana, Steve was "a challenge." As she confided to her psychotherapist, years later, "Steve was this real super-hunk, and I knew Meg was crazy about him. As much as I loved Meg—I mean, she had been my best friend since grade school—I also felt kind of competitive with her." Deana contrived to meet Steve at a restaurant, and wound up taking him back to her apartment. "We sort of ended up in bed," Deana stated, "and I said some real nasty things about Meg. I mean, I told Steve some stuff about Meg that just wasn't true, like that she had a drug problem. I guess I have to admit I wanted to sabotage their relationship." Apparently, Deana succeeded, as she subsequently heard from a very tearful Meg that, "Steve said he doesn't want me to call him again. He wouldn't even say why!" Deana and Meg had not kept in touch over the years; indeed, Meg had moved to another city, though Deana knew her address. Meanwhile, Deana had brooded about her underhanded behavior all these years—and now decided it was time to "make things right." Without discussing the plan with her therapist, Deanna decided to write Meg a letter and confess what had happened between her and Steve. "I wanted to apologize to Meg for, you know, stabbing her in the back that way. And I felt like I really, really needed her forgiveness."

Was Deana living up to the Talmudic principles we have been discussing? Was she being a mensch by "stepping up to the plate" and apologizing to Meg? From the rabbinical perspective, the answer is far from clear. Rabbi Daniel Feldman presents the following rabbinical debate on the matter of apologizing when we have spread damaging information about someone:

> one must also take into consideration those circumstances in which a request for *mechila* [forgiveness] would do more harm than good... R. Yisrael Meir Kagan

[known as Chofetz Chaim, 1838–1933], in his classic work on the laws of *lashon hara* (malicious gossip), rules that one who has spread damaging information about another must seek [the other's] forgiveness, basing his comments on those of Rabbeinu Yonah. [But] R. Yisrael Lipkin (Salanter), revered founder of the modern *Mussar* movement, disagreed, noting that this would require informing the victim, who was until now blissfully ignorant. In inflicting emotional pain, such a gesture would be manifestly counterproductive (Feldman, 1999, 149).

In considering whether to apologize and seek forgiveness from Meg, Deana might need to consider a number of factors. First, Deana and Meg had not been in touch in ten years. How would Meg react to receiving a letter "out of the blue" that resurrected a painful event in the distant past? Second, what real *good* could come out of such a communication? Without knowing Meg's circumstances, it is hard to answer this question. If Meg had married and settled down, with no interest whatsoever in Steve, it is hard to see how any significant good could come of dredging up this "ancient history." On the other hand, if Deana knew that Meg was actually trying to revive her relationship with Steve, it might be important to inform Meg of the lie that Deana had told to Steve. After all, the issue might come up between Meg and Steve, and in those circumstances, Meg should be armed with the facts.

There is another issue to consider. Deana acknowledged that she "*really, really needed [Meg's] forgiveness.*" One wonders if Deana's plan to apologize had more to do with looking out for her *own* needs than those of her erstwhile friend. Confessing some wrong solely to make oneself "feel better" is arguably not an attitude of genuine contrition and repentance. True, one's feeling better may be a desirable *outcome* of such confession—but as a *motive*, it smacks of narcissistic self-involvement. Such a self-centered confession may also suggest a distorted understanding of *honesty*. We will deal in detail with the theme of "Honesty and Integrity" in Chapter 12. But at this point, we should note that in the Judaic tradition, honesty has its time, place, and proper mode of "delivery." While undeniably a foundational value in Judaism, honesty that gratuitously offends, or inflicts pain without a strong countervailing benefit, is not necessarily a virtue. As Telushkin succinctly puts it, "when no constructive purpose is served by being truthful, peace is valued more highly than truth" (Telushkin 2000, 67).

On the other hand, it is easy to invent self-serving rationalizations as to why we should not confess our wrongdoing to those we have hurt. We must always consider if, by *not* asking for forgiveness, we are acting out of a selfish desire to spare ourselves discomfort. As Feldman notes, citing R. David Binyamin Brezacher, "anguish to the victim is sufficient reason to dispense with asking [forgiveness], but...the embarrassment of the offender is not" (Feldman 1999, 150).

PERSONAL ENCOUNTER: THE *CHAFFETZ CHAYYIM* AND ASKING FORGIVENESS

Rabbi Israel Meir Ha-Cohen Kagan (1838–1933) is widely regarded as the foremost Judaic scholar on the matter of *proper speech*—that is, on "guarding one's tongue" (Telushkin 2000, 462). He is generally referred to as the *Chaffetz Chayyim*, meaning "One who desires life," after his most famous book. Rabbi Abraham J. Twerski, M.D., recounts a telling anecdote involving the *Chaffetz Chayyim*, and his incredible capacity for forgiveness (Twerski 2004, xviii). It seems that the rabbi was on his way back home, presumably riding in his buggy, when he saw a man walking on the side of the road. He offered to give the man a lift and asked him where he was going. "To Radin, to see the *Chaffetz Chayyim*," the man replied, obviously not recognizing the great sage. "Why do you want to see him?" asked the *Chaffetz Chayyim*, adding, "There's nothing special about him." The man immediately became enraged at this apparent insult to his beloved *Chaffetz Chayyim*. "How dare you talk about the *Chaffetz Chayyim* like that!" the man shouted, slapping the rabbi in the face. Later, upon arriving in Radin, the man learned that the man he had slapped was the very sage he idolized. He tearfully pleaded with the *Chaffetz Chayyim* for forgiveness. The rabbi smiled and said, "There is nothing to forgive. After all, it was my honor you were defending. But this taught me something. Just as one may not speak *lashon hara* ('evil tongue'), one may not speak *lashon hara* about oneself."

The *Chaffetz Chayyim* very nicely modeled what it means to be a mensch. Obviously, he showed enormous compassion and humility in his forgiveness of the man who had slapped him. But in a sense, the *Chaffetz Chayyim* was also recognizing the need for a kind of *self-forgiveness*. We will say much more on this in Chapter 9 (Respect for Self and Others).

Chapter Eight

Justice and Retribution

You shall not pervert justice; you shall not show partiality; and you shall not take a bribe, for a bribe blinds the eyes of the wise and subverts the cause of the righteous. Justice, and only justice, you shall follow...

—Deuteronomy 16:19–20

A judge who has made a loan from a man on trial may not sit in judgment over him.

—Sanhedrin 105; cited in Newman and Spitz 1945, 220

Where there is harsh justice there is no kindness, and where there is kindness there is no harsh justice! What kind of justice goes hand in hand with kindness? It is: reaching a compromise.

—Sanhedrin 6; cited in ibn Chaviv 1999, 595

Judge everyone by giving him the benefit of the doubt. [When you see a person doing what appears to be wrong, take a favorable view of his action; don't suspect him of wrongdoing (Rashi)].

—Shevuot 30a; cited in ibn Chaviv 1999, 720

Judge not thy neighbor until thou hast put thyself in his place; judge all men charitably.

—Pirke Avot 2:5; cited in Newman and Spitz 1945, 226

Rabbi Dov Peretz Elkins asks us, "Who in life does not, at some time or another, have to pass judgment on the well-being of another, sometimes in serious matters and sometimes in less weighty ones? ...we are all judges at different times in our lives." (Elkins 2007, 66–67). Indeed, in Judaism, the matter of justice is not of merely historical interest; rather, the quest for justice is a vital, driving force in our modern-day lives.

That said, Rabbi Elkins points out an important historical fact: until the development of the Torah, there was no transcendent, religiously-based legal code:

> Codes of law existed in ancient Mesopotamia, but they were based on what was utilitarian, and not on any religious philosophic notion of right and wrong... Along came the Torah, positing an overarching notion of justice that God built into the world. Nothing like this had ever been known before. It was a revolution that changed the world and society forever (Elkins 2007, 65–66).

The Talmud, too, points to *justice* as one of the ethical pillars of Judaism. In Pirke Avot (1:18), Rabban Shimon, the son of Gamliel (i.e., Shimon ben Gamliel II) says: "The world is preserved through three things: truth, justice, and peace." And in another tractate of the Talmud, we are told, "Every judge should see himself as though a sword is about to enter his body, and hell is open at his feet" (Sanhedrin 7b; quoted in Elkins 2007, 65). Elkins notes that "Justice in the Jewish court system is demanded over and over again, and no influence, bribe, or favoritism is ever allowed to enter into the equation of dispensing fair and honest judgment" (Elkins 2007, 65).

But what has all this elevated talk to do with the mensch? To be sure: the mensch may not sit in judgment in a courtroom, or give instructions to a jury. He or she is not likely to sentence another individual to life in prison, much less to death. And yet, each of us passes judgment every day—on our family, friends, workmates, and subordinates. Each of us is tempted, seduced, or "bribed" by factors or events that draw us away from justice. Moreover, each of us renders judgment, nearly every day, regarding how severely we ought to deal with those who wrong us, in word or deed. Each of us passes judgment as to how much we ought to "punish" someone who slights us, speaks ill of us, or sins against us. Seen in this light, justice is something we rise to, or fall from, in our most mundane encounters with the world.

Dean was absolutely thrilled. His grass-roots environmental education group, "GoForGreen," had just been awarded a $5,000 grant from the Environmental Protection Agency, with an additional $5000 in matching funds from a private corporation. The latter monies were "contingent upon appropriate performance of grantee's duties." Dean's proposal called for a series of twenty "town hall meetings" at which Dean and his two colleagues would lecture on matters of local environmental importance. Dean was especially concerned with a plan under consideration by the Town Council that would have eliminated several *acres of wetlands in his community, in order to make way for a new condominium complex. He had planned to discuss the adverse environmental impact of this plan at the first town hall meeting. About a week prior to his scheduled lecture, Dean received a call from the public relations office of the private firm ("Enviro-Tech") that had provided matching funds. Sounding quite friendly and open, a Mr. Andrews suggested that he and Dean might "have dinner some time, just to talk over a few ideas." Although Dean had some qualms about meeting Andrews, he did not see anything inherently wrong in simply "hearing what he has to say" over dinner. However, Dean did not discuss the invitation with either of his two colleagues. After doing some "digging" on the Internet, Dean discovered that Enviro-Tech was the parent company of the firm that was hoping to build the condominium complex. Dean's uneasiness grew, but he did not cancel his dinner meeting. Mr. Andrews arranged to meet Dean at the best restaurant in town. After presenting his "ideas" over a sumptuous meal and an expensive bottle of wine, Andrews insisted on picking up the tab—which came to well over $300. Andrews had not tried to coerce or bribe Dean in any overt fashion—he had merely talked enthusiastically about "the great benefits" the proposed condominium complex would bring to Dean's home town, including many new jobs related to construction.*

Dean sensed that something "fishy" had happened, and left the restaurant feeling very displeased with himself.

So why was Dean feeling so uneasy? The Talmud tells us that, "A judge who has made a loan from a man on trial may not sit in judgment over him" (Sanhedrin 105; cited in Newman and Spitz 1945, 220). Dean was clearly not a "judge" in any formal sense, nor had he received a loan from Andrews—nor was Andrews "on trial." And yet, the Talmudic injunction applies to Dean. After all, Dean had received a *favor* from Andrews and his firm, by way of the matching loan. And Dean had been the beneficiary of an expensive dinner, paid for by Andrews. Furthermore, in a sense, Dean's lecture would be a kind of "judgment" on the entire enterprise Andrews and his firm were undertaking: for example, would the proposed condominiums have an adverse impact on local wildlife, soil and water quality, etc.?

If Dean shaded his true feelings about the condominiums—say, by understating their adverse impact on the environment—Dean would compromise his fiduciary responsibilities to his town, his organization, and the E.P.A. On the other hand, if Dean were honest about the adverse effects of the condos, he might risk alienating the Enviro-Tech—and who knows what that could mean? Perhaps they would not come through with their matching funds; at the very least, they might never support any further ventures on the part of Dean's organization. Dean was in the middle of a classic *conflict of interest—*

or what the Talmud calls, *Nogea B'Davar* ("being an interested party"; see Fogel and Friedman 2008, 238). The Talmud tells us that one who is *Nogea B'Davar* is disqualified from testifying as a witness, because he or she can't be objective—after all, one's own interests are at stake. And if one can't be an objective witness, one certainly can't be an objective judge.

So what is a mensch to do, when placed in such a bind? An answer is suggested in a passage from Maimonides' *Laws of Sanhedrin:* "A judge was once crossing a river on a small boat when a person stretched out his hand and helped the judge to get ashore. When the judge found out that the man who helped him had a case before him, the judge disqualified himself." (23:3; in Quint 1990, 71).

One might say that in Dean's case, Andrews and his company had "stretched out their hand" on two occasions: first, in providing Dean's matching grant money; and second, on treating Dean to a lavish dinner. In addition, Dean's objectivity was compromised by the possibility that if Enviro-Tech was not pleased with his lecture, they might withhold their funding. The course of the mensch in this case is clear: Dean needs to recuse (disqualify) himself from delivering the lecture. Indeed, since Dean's colleagues might also be influenced by the potential withholding of funds by Enviro-Tech, it is doubtful that either of them could speak objectively on the subject of the condominiums.

Bill and Laura arrived home from their vacation to find red "crime scene" tape stretched across their front door. Their house had obviously been vandalized. A police notice, taped to the door, instructed them to contact the investigating officer. The officer informed the couple that a neighborhood youth named Duncan had been charged in the crime, and that the evidence implicating him was very strong. As soon as Laura heard the name, she exclaimed, "But I know Duncan! He's the Lawrence's boy—our neighbors, two doors down. He's not really a bad kid, and I understand that he's been through a lot." Indeed, Duncan was well known in the neighborhood as a shy and withdrawn "loner." He had not been in legal trouble before, though once he had been reprimanded by the police for "egging" a neighbor's house on Halloween. Duncan's parents were also well known in Bill and Laura's small-town neighborhood, mainly for their bad tempers. Duncan's father was often described as a "nasty drunk" who had physically abused Duncan on more than one occasion. In recent months, Bill and Laura learned, Duncan had been counseled in school for possible post-traumatic stress disorder (PTSD), stemming from this abuse. The police officer told Bill and Laura that because Duncan had just turned 18, he was to be prosecuted as an adult—assuming that Bill and Laura wanted to press charges. The damage to their

*home was not trivial: their brand-new entertainment center, worth well over
$1500, had been badly damaged; the living room carpet had been ruined;
and an expensive vase had been smashed.*

So what should a mensch do in a case like this? Obviously, Bill and Laura
have every right to be angry with Duncan, and to insist on prosecution to the
"full extent of the law." Violating the sanctity of someone's home is a serious legal and moral offense, but more than that: it is a painful psychological trauma for the victims. Furthermore, Bill and Laura are under no moral
obligation to "coddle" Duncan, simply because he has experienced parental
abuse: his behavior was inexcusable, and a psychological understanding of
PTSD should not mean a "free pass" for someone who has vandalized another's home! (Not everybody who is physically abused makes a decision to
break the law, after all).

   And yet: the Talmud tells us, *"Where there is harsh justice there is no
kindness, and where there is kindness there is no harsh justice! What kind
of justice goes hand in hand with kindness? It is: reaching a compromise"*
(Sanhedrin 6; in ibn Chaviv 1999, 595).

   Ordinarily, when the Rabbis spoke of "compromise" in the legal sense,
they had in mind a process of *arbitration [*Hebrew*, peshara]*, in which two
parties in a civil suit—each, perhaps, with some merit to his claim—would
agree to a process of mediation by the court or *beth din* (Quint 1990, 91–99).
In the case of Duncan's vandalism, we are speaking of an obvious *criminal*
offense. It is not as if Duncan has a compelling argument in his own behalf,
such as claiming a right to his act of intrusion and vandalism.

   But in weighing their own role in the matter, Laura and Bill should consider another principle in the Talmud known as *lifnim meshurat hadin*—essentially, "going beyond the letter of the law" (Telushkin 2000, 290). Let's
be clear: the Rabbis were *not* insisting that we give up a legal claim that is
rightfully ours. But they were asking that we temper our legal claims with
mercy. And so the Talmud asks, "Whose sin is forgiven? The sin of him who
forgives sins [committed against himself or herself]" (Megillah 28a; cited in
Telushkin 2000, 290). Indeed, as we discussed in the preceding chapter on
"Forgiveness," the Talmud warns that one who refuses to forgive is called
akhzari, "cruel" (Bava Kama 92a; Feldman 1999, 151). Here we see how
forgiveness and mercy are inseparable from the Talmudic concept of justice
and retribution. As Rabbi Ben Zion Bokser eloquently states the matter,

   Those actions "beyond the line of the law"…constituted a free zone in which individuals expressed their generosity and love for their fellow men, without com-
   pulsion from outside sources. The Talmud hailed this free zone of moral action
   as the very foundation of a good society. A community in which…[individuals]

are content to hew to the strict letter of the law was devoid of the moral cement that gives a social order stability and enables it to survive (Bokser, 2001, 145).

In light of the "generosity" envisioned by the principle of *lifnim meshurat hadin*, what might be the most humane position for Bill and Laura to take with respect to Duncan's misdeed? What would a mensch do in these circumstances?

When all parties came before the court in a preliminary hearing, Bill and Laura decided not to press charges against Duncan, if certain conditions were met by Duncan and his family. First, Duncan would apologize for his behavior, and agree to compensate Bill and Laura for damages—an amount their insurance company set at $3200. Second, Duncan would agree to perform some type of community service, to be determined by the court. Third, Duncan's father would agree to attend "anger management" counseling and a 12-step program, aimed at curbing his abusive behaviors and alcohol abuse. Finally, Duncan and his parents would also agree to attend family counseling sessions, in order to deal with the underlying issues that might be fueling Duncan's misbehavior. The judge in the case agreed with this plan, as did Duncan's lawyer and parents. After the hearing was over, Duncan met with Bill and Laura. He seemed genuinely remorseful about his vandalism, and apologized to Bill and Laura for the grief he had caused them.

This vignette is not intended to present an accurate depiction of the American legal system, which probably operates in a far less nuanced way most of the time. Nor is it intended to convey the notion that we ought to let lawbreakers "off the hook" in some reflexive and unthinking manner. Rather, it is intended to depict the *dialectical* relationship of justice and mercy in Judaism—a theme explored in detail by law professor and rabbi Samuel J. Levine (Levine 2007, 455–70). Although strict adherence to the law *is* articulated as a virtue in the Talmud (see, e.g., Sanhedrin 6b), this attitude is balanced by the requirement for *kindness and mercy*. Levine draws on the views of the preeminent Orthodox rabbi, Joseph B. Soloveitchik (1903–93) to make this point. Rabbi Soleveitchik writes that, in the exercise of *peshara* (arbitration, compromise),

social harmony is the main concern of the judge. The fine points of the law and the determination of precise facts are of secondary importance. The goal is not to be juridically astute but to be socially healing. The psychology of the contenders, their socio-economic status and values, as well as the general temper of society, are the primary ingredients employed in the *peshara* process. These considerations are evaluated within the broad [legal] parameters of the [codes] and the final resolution of the conflict is a delicate and sensitive blending of both objective legal norms and subjective humanistic goals. For this reason, *peshara* is the preferred alternative (from Besdin 1981, *Reflections of the Rav: Lessons in Jewish Thought*, cited in Levine 2007, 466–7).

The need for mercy as a component of justice is wonderfully expressed in a section of the Talmud that describes what *God* prays for—and yes, in the Talmud, even God prays! Here is what Rabbi Zutra ben Tobi says in the name of Rav:

> What does God pray?...[He prays] "May it be My will that My mercy may suppress My anger, and that My mercy shall prevail over My attributes of justice and of recompense; that I may deal with My children in the attribute of mercy and, stopping well short of the line of strict justice, acting for their well-being." (Berakhot 7a; cited in Borowitz and Schwartz 1999, 73).

Lou and Heshie ran a small discount furniture store and had been business partners for 30 years. Lou "kept the books," while Heshie took care of sales and advertising. Although they did not often socialize, Lou and Heshie considered themselves "friends" and had always gotten along well. Once, when Lou was sick, Heshie "covered" for him in the store, basically running the place by himself for nearly three weeks. But one day, the office secretary took Lou aside and whispered to him nervously, "Please don't tell Heshie this, Lou, but I think he's been cooking the books lately." Lou had an independent accounting firm go over the books and found that, indeed, Heshie had been pocketing a few hundred dollars here and there, over the last three months or so. Prior to that, the accounting firm found no irregularities at all. Lou was initially very upset and angry. For several days, he brooded about taking Heshie to small claims court and parting ways with him. On the other hand, Lou had considered Heshie a friend for more than thirty years and wondered if perhaps something had come up for Heshie in the past three months. Lou decided to speak privately with Heshie and avoid making any accusations. During a private meeting over lunch, Lou asked Heshie "how things were going at home." Heshie looked stricken, and began to sob softly. "Esther (his wife) found out she needs a bone marrow transplant—she's got some kind of leukemia, Lou. Our health insurance coverage lapsed years ago, and we haven't been able to get a new policy at a price we can afford. I didn't want to beg—so I thought maybe I could just skim a little off the top...you know, to help pay for the operation."

By all legal measures, Heshie was committing larceny, and could easily have been prosecuted, had Lou chosen to bring charges against him. Instead, Lou chose to forgive Heshie and worked out a repayment plan for the five hundred or so dollars Heshie had stolen. Furthermore, since Lou's company did not provide health insurance for its small group of employees, Lou decided to loan Heshie several thousand dollars, to cover the cost of Esther's operation.

Lou was not necessarily conscious of the teaching from Pirke Avot that says, "Judge not thy neighbor until thou hast put thyself in his place; judge all men charitably" (Pirke Avot 2:5; cited in Newman and Spitz 1945, 226). However, Lou's actions suggest that he was living out the spirit of this teaching.

Commenting on Pirke Avot 2:5, the great medieval commentator Rabbi Shlomo Yitzchaki (1040–1105 C.E.), better known as Rashi, taught as follows: "Do not harshly condemn a person who succumbed to temptation until, faced by a similar temptation, you overcame it" (cited in Hertz 1952, 27).

Pirke Avot 1:6, on the other hand, is sometimes open to slight misinterpretation. It is often translated (in part) as, "Judge all individuals charitably" or paraphrased as "Give everyone the benefit of the doubt." But as Rabbi Joseph Telushkin writes, this is not quite what the Hebrew says:

> In truth, the accurate translation of the rabbinic proverb is "Judge *the whole* of a person favorably." In other words, when you assess another, do not rely exclusively on one or two bad things you know about the person; be influenced by the good things you know as well, particularly if they are more significant... [moreover] when you know a person to be largely good, and subsequently learn that he or she has done something wrong, you should not rush to condemn that individual. Rather, try to understand why the person acted as he did, and consider possible excuses for his behavior" (Telushkin 2000, 36, italics added).

It's fair to say that, faced with an act that might have led many to harsh retribution, Lou acted in concert with both teachings (2:5, 1:6) from Pirke Avot. Indeed, Lou acted like a real mensch!

The Talmud does not require merely that we refrain from injustice, or even merely that we judge others fairly; rather, we are required to *protest injustice*, in a vocal and active manner. Rabbi Joseph Telushkin cites the Biblical story of how Moses struck an Egyptian overseer, when the latter had been brutally whipping an Israelite (Telushkin 2000, 87). Indeed, Moses struck the overseer so hard that the man died. Perhaps this example of "standing up for justice" is atypical in the rabbinical tradition, since—as Rabbi Telushkin points out—Moses was "overcome with anger" (Telushkin 2007, 87). We have already seen that, in general, the Rabbis are eager to avoid anger of such proportions. Nevertheless, passivity in the face of injustice is neither the way of Judaism, nor the way of the mensch.

Rob was the manager of a large discount store that was part of a huge national chain. Rob's first priority, understandably, was "keeping the customer satisfied" and "watching the bottom line" in very difficult financial times. But Rob was bothered by some practices and policies that he was asked to oversee, at the behest of the national chain's corporate management. For example, Rob was told by his superiors that any mandatory overtime on the part of his employees "should not be compensated as such." Rob also noticed that when he promoted females to a higher level of authority, the national management frequently questioned his decision, and in one case, countermanded the promotion. This left one of his best female employees furious with Rob, and threatening him with legal action. Rob decided that he would join the employee in a complaint to the national office, hoping to resolve the issue out of court.

The Talmud was arguably one of the earliest proponents of fair labor practices in the history of legal and moral codes. As Rabbi Morris Adler points out,

> The Talmud, centuries in advance of general usage, sets a limit upon the hours which one may be required to work. Laborers were permitted to join together and set a wage scale which employers could be asked to meet...[and] a laborer's salary was not to be cut during the period of his absence by reason of illness (Adler 1963, 112).

The Talmud even set standards for the quality of food an employer was to provide for the laborers! Of course, the Talmud also places responsibilities on the laborer; e.g., to perform competently and "not to spend his leisure in a way to make himself unfit to meet the demands of his assignment" (Adler 1963, 113).

Rob's willingness to fight for his employee's promotion was the mark of a mensch. At the same time, the Talmud would ask *more* of Rob and others in his position; for example, Rob should work to change the national chain's unfair labor practices, not merely one employee's job status.

A modern example of Talmudic influence on labor practice is the recent criticism of the nation's largest kosher meatpacking plant, which came under fire for alleged exploitation of workers and lax safety standards (Preston 2008). This has given rise to a new campaign known as *Hekhsher Tzadek* ("justice certification"), which aims to ensure that kosher meatpacking plants follow ethical labor practices.

PERSONAL ENCOUNTER: RABBI AKIBA, FREE WILL, AND GOOD DEEDS

One of the philosophical cornerstones of justice—both in the Judeo-Christian and the Anglo-Saxon traditions—is the principle that human beings exercise some considerable degree of free will. After all, our advocating virtuous action would make little sense if we did not believe ourselves "free" on some level to choose good over evil. Nor would our system of reward and punishment have any moral basis. And yet, in Judaism, free will exists in a kind of dynamic tension with *God's omniscience*. God has before Him all possible knowledge of all events, even those that have yet to occur; and yet, we are free to choose. Nowhere in the Talmud is this more forcefully stated than in Pirke Avot 3:19, when the great Rabbi Akiba ben Joseph (ca 50–132 C.E.) states, "All is foreseen, yet freedom [of choice] is given."

But who was this Akiba ben Joseph? His youth and much of his life are the stuff of legend, but this much seems probable: Akiba was a poor and uneducated shepherd who, in his later years, decided to enter the rabbinical academy. He proceeded to systematize the still chaotic teachings of the Talmud, as Rabbi Louis Ginzberg (2008) notes: "Akiba made the accumulated treasure of the oral law—which until his time was only a subject of knowledge, and not a science—an inexhaustible mine from which...new treasures might be continually extracted."

Indeed, Ginzberg believes that Akiba, "to a degree beyond any other, deserves to be called the father of rabbinical Judaism" (Ginzberg 2002). Legend has it that Rabbi Akiba supported the rebellion of Shimon Bar Kokhba against Roman dominion, and that he died a martyr at the hands of the Romans. But Ginzberg argues that it was not for *political* reasons that Akiba was executed; rather, "he suffered martyrdom on account of his transgression of Hadrian's edicts against the practice and the teaching of the Jewish religion" (Ginzberg 2002).

The first part of Rabbi Akiba's teaching in Pirke Avot 3:19, regarding freedom of the will, is very well known. Perhaps less discussed is the second portion of his teaching; i.e., that "everything is in accordance with the abundance of one's [good] deeds" (Davis 2002, 56). One interpretation of this is that, "Man is condemned or acquitted according to the *preponderance* of his good or bad deeds" (Davis 2002, 56). This concept has important implications for how we judge both ourselves and others. It was expressed eloquently by the medieval German monk, Thomas a Kempis, who said, "You are a man, not God; you are human, not an angel. How can you expect to remain always in a constant state of virtue, when this was not possible even for an angel of Heaven, nor for the first man in the Garden?" (a Kempis 1995, 176).

This philosophy—from Akiba to a Kempis—also informs the psychology of the late Dr. Albert Ellis, the founder of Rational-Emotive Therapy. Ellis reminds us that "Lack of forgiveness toward others breeds lack of self-forgiveness, with consequent perfectionistic attitudes toward one's own failings and incompetencies" (Ellis and Harper 1975, 105).

In short: a mensch is one who accepts personal responsibility for his actions, but who judges both himself and others fairly and comprehensively. As Shakespeare's Hamlet puts it, speaking of his late father, "He was a man, take him for all in all…" (Hamlet, Act 1 scene 2).

Chapter Nine

Respect for Self and Others

He [Hillel the Elder] used to say, "If I am not for myself, who is for me? When I am for myself only, what am I? And if not now, when?"

—Pirke Avot 1:14

Rabbi Shimon says... "do not consider yourself wicked."

—Pirke Avot 2:18

A person is not permitted to harm himself or herself

—Bava Kamma 8:6; cited in Telushkin 2000, 115

Whoever destroys a soul, it is considered as if he destroyed an entire world. And whoever saves a life, it is considered as if he saved an entire world.

—Jerusalem Talmud, Sanhedrin 4:1 (22a)

Great is human dignity, so much so that it overpowers a prohibition of the Torah.

—Berakhot 19b; cited in Feldman 1999, 189

If you did a little harm to your neighbor, let it be in your eyes as if it were much. And if you did a great good to your neighbor, let it be in your eyes as if it were only a little.

—Avot d'Rabbi Natan 41:11; cited in Elkins 2007, 22

Whoever shames another in public is like one who sheds blood.

—Bava Metzia 58b; cited in Elkins 2007, 20

Respect for oneself and others lies at the very heart of Judaism. This extends not only to the preservation of *life and bodily well being*; but also to the *emotional and spiritual well being* of oneself and others.

The astute reader may sense that there is considerable overlap between the value of "respect" and other values we have discussed or will discuss; for example, *kindness, generosity, humility, attentiveness, and politeness.* Indeed, in some sense, all these attributes of the mensch could be subsumed under Hillel's famous synopsis of the Talmud. When provoked by a heathen to define Judaism's essence while standing on one foot, Hillel replied: "What's hateful unto you, don't do unto your neighbor. The rest is commentary. Now, go and study." (Shabbat 31a, cited in Telushkin 2000, 218). Although this Judaic formulation of the "Golden Rule" is stated in terms of what *not* to do, it clearly points the mensch toward the virtue of respect for others.

The need to respect *oneself*, however, is also paramount in Judaism. Hillel's famous question, "*If I am not for myself, who is for me?*" (in Hebrew, *"Im ein ani li, mi li?"*) has been interpreted in many different ways. For example, Rabbi Moshe Lieber's interpretation is, "If I am not concerned for my own spiritual health, who will be concerned for it?" (Lieber 1995, 42). Rabbi Berel Wein's understanding is somewhat more down-to-earth: "A person's primary duty is to oneself, one's personal welfare, and one's family" (Wein 2003, 39). These and many other interpretations no doubt apply, but I believe Hillel was also talking about the need for self-respect, and its relation to earning the respect of others. In short, it is the mensch's task to understand the *dialectical* nature of self-respect and respect for others: without the first, the second becomes nearly impossible. But self-regard alone—without caring for others—reduces us to a "what" instead of a "who."

Meg was known in the office as "Little Miss Doormat." At 33 years of age, Meg was clearly a very bright, capable and hard-working employee. As the personal secretary to Jennifer—a high-powered executive in the company— Meg was the real organizing force in the office. As one of her workmates put it, "If you want something done right, you go to Meg. Without her, the whole place would fall apart." But despite this positive assessment, most of the office staff took advantage of Meg. Several of the mid-level executives would pile work on Meg's desk, even though—officially—Meg worked only for Jennifer. Meg would usually "suck it up" (as she put it), rather than "making problems for myself." If Jennifer told Meg to stay late in order to meet a typing deadline, Meg would do so without complaint, even when it meant missing dinner with her family. Even at home, Meg felt that, "I usually get the short end of the stick." For example, her husband would expect Meg to make dinner, even when she got home late. "Sometimes, Rick has already been home for an hour, by the time I get there, but he hasn't lifted a finger. I mean, you'd think he could pick up something at the deli, or maybe even heat up something from the freezer, for goodness sake!" Yet despite her dissatisfaction with Rick's behavior, Meg never raised the issue with him. "Look, I don't want to make trouble," Meg explained. "Rick is basically a good guy. I mean, it's not like he beats me or cheats on me. It's just—well, I wish he'd see that I need some help now and then." As for Rick, he professed his love for Meg, but added, "Sometimes it's just hard to relate to Meg as a real person. I mean, she just seems to live through others. She's a good woman and a good wife, but sometimes I wish she'd stand up for herself and tell me what she really wants from our marriage."

Meg is undoubtedly a decent, good-hearted person, but she is clearly not "for herself," in Rabbi Hillel's terms. In the long run, such passive behavior creates risks. As a Yiddish proverb succinctly states, "He who puts up with insult invites injury" (Stone 2006, 234). Let me be clear: we must not blame the victim for such abuse. Acting like a "doormat" does not justify the selfish, disrespectful or abusive behavior of others. But the reality is that many people *will* take advantage of passive and unassertive people like Meg, sometimes to the point of inflicting emotional or even physical injury.

Furthermore, those who do not stand up for themselves make it hard for others to appreciate them. As the neo-orthodox rabbi, Samson Raphael Hirsch (1808–88) counseled, "First, become a blessing to yourself, so that you may be a blessing to others." (Gross and Gross 1992, 169). Self-esteem must lay the foundation for the esteem of others. Meg's husband is clearly expressing how hard it is to see Meg as a fully-formed individual—as a mensch! Meg's lack of assertiveness and self-respect reminds me a bit of the character Bontsha Schweig ("Bontsha the Silent"), in the story by Isaac Loeb Peretz (1852–1915). Although Bontsha has been praised by some readers as a model of humility, many have seen his behavior in more negative terms. As an Israeli commentator recently put it, in a political context: "For too long, Israelis have been imprisoned in the 'Bontsha Schweig' mentality, as in the Yiddish story 'Bontsha the Silent,' where all the little Jew demanded after a lifetime of humiliations was a hot buttered roll" (Troy 2003).

We needn't endorse the political views of the editorial to understand the point about Bontsha—and by analogy, about Meg.

Jess was a junior in high school when he started to feel depressed, though he didn't use that term. "It's like, what's the point?" he would write to one of his "friends" on a popular website for teenagers. "I'm such a loser. I'll never find a girl and I'll never figure out what I want to do with my life."

Jess was judged to be very bright by his teachers, but had gotten into some serious trouble, both in and out of school. When he was thirteen, Jess and a group of friends were required to perform community service after being caught knocking down parking meters while drunk. When he was fifteen, Jess was suspended from school for swearing at the guidance counselor. Jess's parents tried to talk with him, but, as his mother put it, "Jess is just shut down. He just tells me to get out of his room." Jess's parents had been advised to "get counseling" for Jess and the family, but Jess refused to go. Recently, he had begun frequenting a local tattoo parlor, which had once been closed by the Board of Health for using unsanitary needles. Even worse, Jess had begun using a razor blade to make small cuts on his arms, usually after "getting high." "It's the only time I really feel alive," Jess wrote to his email contact. He added, "I know I'm not worth all the trouble I put people through, dude. I'm like, a waste of space. Not sure how much longer I want to go on like this, man."

It is clear that Jess is in very serious trouble. Most likely, he is suffering from some type of clinical depression, though the turmoil of adolescence is sometimes hard to distinguish from depression. Certainly, Jess's drug abuse, self-injuring behavior, and veiled allusion to ending his life suggest a pathological condition rather than "normal adolescent angst," and should be addressed urgently. Nobody should "blame" Jess for the way he feels—though he needs to be held accountable for his misbehavior—and he would benefit from some kind of psychotherapy, and perhaps even medication.

But there is a spiritual dimension to Jess's suffering that is also worth our attention, and which bears on the conduct of the mensch. It is summed up in the two teachings we cited at the beginning of this section; i.e., "Rabbi Shimon says...'do not consider yourself wicked' " (Pirke Avot 2:18); and, "A person is not permitted to harm himself or herself" (Bava Kamma 8:6; cited in Telushkin 2000, 115).

Now, no one with a modicum of good sense would approach Jess by saying, "Hey, kid, read the Talmud! It says you shouldn't hate yourself or cut yourself!" That sort of bull-in-a-china-shop approach may be worse than doing nothing. As the psychotherapist Frieda Fromm-Reichmann once said, "The patient needs an experience, not an explanation" (Curtis 2009, 119). That experience needs to take place in a setting of *safety, trust,* and *empathy*—for example, in some form of counseling or therapy. Through a process that may take weeks, months, or longer, Jess's way of thinking about himself may gradually come to change.

However, many of us with less malignant forms of self-loathing or self-injury can make direct use of the Talmud's insights. Many people who constantly put themselves down, or who fail to take good care of themselves, can benefit from what the rabbis have to teach us.

Self-respect begins, fundamentally, with respect for one's body, the practice of taking care of our bodies, of *shemirat haguf* (Rosenberg 2003, 48). As Bokser tells us (2001, 136), "The Talmud urged the proper care of the body as an obligation which one owes toward himself...the Rabbis looked upon the maintenance of bodily health as a religious obligation." Indeed, Rabbi Bokser quotes Hillel as saying, "Surely must I, who am created in the divine image and likeness, take care of my body!" (Leviticus Rabbah 34:*3*; cited in Bokser 2001, 136).

The Talmud makes it clear that we are not to harm our bodies either directly or indirectly, and that unnecessary risk taking is prohibited. Thus, we read in the name of Resh Lakish that "a Torah scholar may not afflict himself by fasting [voluntarily] because [he becomes weak] and is unable to learn Torah" (Taanit 10b; in ibn Chaviv 1999, 300).

Similarly, Maimonides wrote extensively on the proper care of the body (and soul). The driving force behind Rambam's exhortations, however, was not the achievement of good health for its own sake. Rather, as with Resh Lakish, good health is merely a means toward the end of serving God. As Rambam puts it,

> Since preserving the body's health and strength is among the ways of the Lord—for to attain understanding and knowledge is impossible when one is sick—a man needs to keep away from things that destroy the body, and to accustom himself to things that make him healthy and vigorous (*Laws Concerning Character Traits*, chapter 4; cited in Weiss and Butterworth 1983, 36).

Maimonides also laid out very specific guidelines for healthy diet, sleep, and sexual activity—the guiding principle being one of *moderation* (see Chapter 5).

What about Jess's allusion to ending his life? Aside from the psychological issues involved, what does the Talmud have to say on the matter? Admittedly, there is some debate on this matter, as it is not precisely clear that the Talmud explicitly prohibits suicide (see Gittin 57b and comments of Rabbi Yosef Shaul Nathanson, cited in Feldman 1999, 16). For example, some rabbinical opinion would hold that the 960 Jews who killed themselves and their families at Masada in 73 C.E. may have been prompted by the justifiable desire to avoid being sold off as slaves and prostitutes (Telushkin 1994, 274). Nevertheless, except perhaps in the most extraordinary and extreme circumstances, suicide is prohibited in Judaism; indeed, it is regarded as a kind of murder (Telushkin 2000, 260).

Similarly, self-injury or self-mutilation is prohibited by the Rabbis, based on the statement in the Torah, "You shall not...incise any marks on yourselves" (Leviticus 19:28; cited in Telushkin 2000, 260). This would generally preclude any tattoos that involve the use of needles. While there is some debate in the rabbinical literature regarding cosmetic "body piercing" (nose rings, earrings, etc.), Rabbi Chaim Steinmetz concludes that "If the body piercing is done solely for the sake of beauty, there would be a debate about its permissibility. However, if it is done to associate with a subculture of masochism and self-destruction, it would violate the prohibition against wounding" (Steinmetz, n.d.).

In short, the mensch values and respects his or her bodily health and avoids anything that needlessly compromises one's health and safety. That said, there may be times when a person must take substantial risks in order to fulfill a professional obligation. We will explore this issue in our next vignette.

Mitch was a nurse practitioner working at a health clinic in New Orleans, just prior to Hurricane Katrina. On Monday, August 29th, 2005, just hours before Hurricane Katrina made landfall, the 17th Street Canal levee was breached, and the neighborhood slowly began to flood. Later that morning, Mitch and a nurse colleague, Sarah, made their way to the health clinic, which abutted on the area near the breach, to make sure that any patients who might come in would be helped to safety. There were only five patients scheduled that morning, and—by making a series of phone calls—Mitch and Sarah determined that all but one had been evacuated to safety the day before. The remaining patient, a Mrs. Stover, lived alone and suffered from a variety of physical and emotional problems. Calls to her apartment produced no response, and Mitch and Sarah began to fear the worst. After several unsuccessful attempts to contact the local police and Red Cross, Mitch and Sarah called a friend who lived in the neighborhood and had a small boat. The three of them set out in the boat, rowing through flooded sections of the neighborhood, finally reaching Mrs. Stover's apartment building. The first floor had already been flooded, and Mrs. Stover was sitting on her second floor balcony, weeping softly. Mitch and Sarah were able to climb on to the balcony and eventually were able to move Mrs. Stover into the boat. The three of them ultimately found safety at a Red Cross shelter.

Earlier, in reference to Jess, we discussed the Talmudic injunction to safeguard our own bodily well being. But there are times when risking one's life to save another is also a *mitzvah*—and certainly, an attribute of the mensch. We are told, *"Whoever destroys a soul, it is considered as if he destroyed an entire world. And whoever saves a life, it is considered as if he saved an entire world"* (Jerusalem Talmud, Sanhedrin 4:1 [22a]).

In the Talmud, the principle of *pikuach nefesh* ("danger to life") overrides all religious laws except those involving murder, idolatry, and prohibited sexual unions (Kottek 1997, 25). As our vignette suggests, a special responsibility for preserving life rests upon the shoulders of physicians, nurses, and allied health professionals; indeed, in Talmudic times, the physician was regarded as a representative or "messenger" of the Lord (Kottek 1997, 24). However, the duty to take *reasonable risks* to save the life of another extends to *all* individuals. In the Bible, we are admonished, "Do not stand by while your neighbor's blood is shed" (Leviticus 19:16). Based on this verse, the Talmud instructs us that if we see someone drowning, being mauled by animals, or being attacked by robbers, we must do our best to save the person (Babylonian Talmud, Sanhedrin 73a; Telushkin 2000, 120–1).

On the other hand, the Rabbis did not wish or expect us to become martyrs, in order to save another's life. In fact, in a famous Talmudic dilemma involving two men in the desert with enough water only for one to survive, the revered sage, Rabbi Akiva argues in favor of *self-preservation*; i.e., if it comes down to one's own survival or that of another, one is entitled to put his own life first (Bava Mezia 62a; Telushkin 2000, 298–9). Far be it from me to disagree with Rabbi Akiva! Nevertheless, even if one drinks all the water in these dire circumstances, one is still obligated to do as much for one's companion as possible. For example, one might try to carry his companion on his shoulders, in hopes that the two of them might come upon a third party who could render assistance. In any case, there is nothing in this Talmudic conundrum that precludes such a possibility (see Cardozo 2004).

Sam and Herb, both businessmen in their 40s, were good friends as well as neighbors. The two had known each other since college and had shared good times and bad. Their families often got together for dinners, outings, barbecues, and ball games. Sam knew that Herb had suffered periodic bouts of depression over the years, but the topic rarely came up, since Herb seemed reluctant to discuss it. One day, Herb mentioned to Sam that he was a little anxious about a business trip he needed to make the following week, since he had a poor sense of direction and would have to drive in a part of the city that he did not know well. Sam immediately offered to lend Herb his new global positioning device, which Herb could easily install in his own car. Herb seemed grateful and promised to return the device right after the trip. Unfortunately, and unbeknownst to Sam, Herb developed what was later diagnosed as a "manic episode," shortly after their meeting. Herb wound up being stopped by the police for driving in an erratic fashion and winding up in a ditch. Since he was judged to be psychotic, the police brought Herb to a local emergency room, and he was subsequently hospitalized for three weeks.

After his discharge, Herb did not seem to realize that, in the confusion of his manic episode, he had lost Sam's global positioning device. In fact, Herb had no recollection at all of having been given the device (not an uncommon experience, after manic episodes). Sam found out about Herb's psychotic episode indirectly, after Herb's wife mentioned it (with great embarrassment) to Sam's wife. Sam decided not to say anything about the missing device, feeling that it would be a humiliation to his friend. Instead, he asked Herb's wife if there was anything he could do to help.

The Talmud teaches us, "Great is human dignity, so much so that it overpowers a prohibition of the Torah" (Berakhot 19b; cited in Feldman 1999, p.189). The concept of *k'vod habriyot*—usually translated as "human dignity" or "respect for persons"—is one of the cornerstones of Judaic ethics. Under the strictest interpretation, *k'vod habriyot* is applied only when a *rabbinical* (rather than a Biblical) commandment is involved; and only when the dignity of the *majority*, rather than an individual, is at stake (Feldman 1999, 192–3). However, interpreted more broadly, *k'vod habriyot* may apply when only two individuals are involved, and there is an issue of forgiveness (*mechilah*). The principle is that of *forgiving that to which one is entitled by religious law*, in order to safeguard another's dignity. As Rabbi Daniel Feldman puts it, no mensch "would stand on his rights if it meant degradation to another" (Feldman 1999, 193). Sam was evidently reasoning in this way when he did not press his case with Herb. Under Judaic law, of course, an individual has a right to have lost property returned, but in this case, bringing up the issue of the lost device would likely have been humiliating to Herb. Sam was behaving like a mensch, and applying the principles of *mechilah* and *k'vod habriyot*. This kindness, of course, does not eliminate Herb's obligation to return or replace the lost equipment once he is made aware of the loss. There may come a time when the issue could gently and tactfully be raised with Herb—so long as his dignity would not be injured.

Importantly, as Feldman points out, the principle of *k'vod habriyot* applies to *all* persons, not just Jews. This stems from the belief that all human beings are created in the Divine image (Feldman 1999, 192).

Another worthwhile teaching to govern the behavior of friends and neighbors: "If you did a little harm to your neighbor, let it be in your eyes as if it were much. And if you did a great good to your neighbor, let it be in your eyes as if it were only a little" (Avot d'Rabbi Natan 41:11; cited in Elkins 2007, 22).

Sandy and Beth were co-chairs of the fundraising committee for their church. This year's goal was to raise at least $5,000 to help families who had suffered *losses as a result of the Iraq War. Both Sandy and Beth were diligent in circulating fliers, appealing to the congregation, and arranging a bake sale to raise money. After two months of hard work, they succeeded in raising nearly $6,000, some of which was in cash. Unfortunately, Beth—whose husband had been severely injured in Afghanistan and who now faced enormous medical expenses—had pocketed $300 of the monies. Sandy knew this, since she had actually observed Beth take the cash and stuff the bills in her purse. Rather than report this to their pastor, Sandy arranged to meet privately with Beth. Sandy gently confronted Beth regarding the theft, adding, "I know that you and Greg (Beth's husband) have been going through some terrible times, and that Greg's medical expenses are going through the roof. But I'd like you to return that money now, Beth." Beth tearfully agreed, and thanked Sandy for not going to the pastor with the information. The next day, Beth handed Sandy a check for $350—fifty dollars more than she had stolen.*

The Talmud views the public humiliation or shaming of another human being as a sin tantamount to murder, or spilling blood. We are told, "Whoever shames another in public is like one who sheds blood" (Bava Metzia 58b; cited in Elkins, 2007, 20). The image of *bloodshed* is physiologically apt and psychologically astute, since the one who is publicly humiliated typically *blanches* rather than blushes. Indeed, the prophet Isaiah longed for the day that, "Jacob [i.e., the Hebrew people] shall no longer be ashamed, neither shall his face go pale" (Isaiah, 29:22; cited in Borowitz and Schwartz 1999, 192). As Rabbi Dov Peretz Elkins (2007, 20) puts it, "The Rabbis were extraordinarily diligent about preserving the self-respect and dignity of others...Psychological harm, they correctly understood, was as bad, and sometimes worse, than physical harm."

In this case, rather than shame Beth before the pastor or the congregation, Sandy acted like a mensch, and confronted Beth gently and privately. Maimonides (Rambam) would have approved wholeheartedly. He tells us that

> Whoever rebukes his fellow man, whether concerning matters between the two of them or between him [the fellow man] and God, needs to rebuke him in private. He shall speak to him calmly and gently, and make known to him that he talks to [the other person] only for his own good (*Laws Concerning Character Traits*, chapter 6; in Weiss and Butterworth 1983, 48).

PERSONAL ENCOUNTER: RAV SHLOMO ZALMAN AUERBACH AND RESPECT FOR THE LESS FORTUNATE

Rabbi (Rav) Shlomo Zalman Auerbach (1910–1995) was, in Telushkin's words, "one of the great rabbinic scholars of the twentieth century...famous for the compassion and consideration he showed orphans, widows, and others whom society often neglects and ignores" (Telushkin 2000, 109). A lifelong resident of Jerusalem, Rav Shlomo Zalman was revered by his students for his gentle and respectful ways. As one source observed, "When [Rav Shlomo Zalman] had to reprimand students, he did so in his uniquely pleasant and genial way. Because his students loved and respected him, his soft-spoken words had a tremendous impact" (Sofer, n.d.).

In his biography of Rav Shlomo Zalman, Rabbi Hanoch Teller relates a remarkable encounter between the great sage and the parents of a child with apparent mental retardation (cited in Telushkin 2000, 109–10). The boy's parents told Rav Zalman that they were considering two institutions for their son, and they wanted to get the rabbi's opinion on which would be preferable. After listening to the parents describe the two facilities, the rabbi asked, "Where is the boy? What does he say about all this?" The parents looked dumbfounded—they had never even considered discussing the matter with their son, whom they believed incapable of understanding the issue. Rav Shlomo Zalman was irate at what he regarded as a sin against the soul of the child, and insisted on seeing the boy. The astonished parents quickly complied and brought the boy, Akiva, before Rav Zalman. After introducing himself, Rav Zalman said to the boy, "You are going to enter a special school now, and I would like you to represent me and look after all of the religious matters in your new home...I shall now give you *semicha*, which makes you a rabbi, and I want you to use this honor wisely" (Telushkin 2000, 109–10). By all accounts, young Akiva diligently fulfilled his "rabbinical" obligations at the institution—all because a great but gentle soul had shown him kindness and respect.

Chapter Ten

Attentive Listening and Understanding

Incline your ear and hear the words of the wise

—Proverbs 22:17

Incline your ear, and come to me; hear, that your soul may live.

—Isaiah 55:3

From the Forty-eight qualities for acquiring Torah: …"attentive listening"

—Pirke Avot 6:6

A fence for wisdom is silence…

—Rabbi Akiva (Pirke Avot 3:17)

Man has two ears but only one tongue, suggesting that his speech ought to be little and his hearing much.

—Simeon ben Zemah Duran; cited in Golden 1957, 75

Orhot Tzaddikim, the anonymous 16th century work, observes, "There is nothing as good in all the world as listening" (cited in Borowitz and Schwartz 1999, 205). One reason that "attentive listening" is stressed in the Talmud (Pirke Avot 6:6) is that without it, the profound emotional and intellectual link between one generation of Torah scholars and the next would be broken. As Rabbi Irving M. Bunim observes,

If you only write something down for others to read, you may still be misunderstood. Tell, explain, teach the one who will take your place in the next generation. So must a pupil go to a teacher to study, and he must listen with open ears and open heart, if he is to be a link in our unbroken chain of responsible Torah scholars (Bunim 1966, 329).

But attentive listening should not be a trait limited to Torah scholars and their students! It is a quality *all* of us must cultivate if we are to achieve *menschlichkeit*. Indeed, "A recurrent complaint of our prophets is that our biblical ancestors failed to [listen attentively]" (Borowitz and Schwartz 1999, 205). In this age of email abbreviations and text messaging, when we are reduced to typing "MIHYAP!" for "May I have your attention, please!" our ability to listen attentively has been sorely tested.

Janet was a high school teacher with nearly twenty years' experience. Although she loved her subject—World History—Janet was feeling "a little burned out" in recent years. As the school budget had shrunk, and classes had expanded, the pressures of teaching had started to wear Janet down. Once, at the end of a long and frustrating day, one of Janet's best students, a young man named Brandon, knocked on the classroom door. Janet was tired and nearly ready to head home, but she could hardly ignore Brandon. The young man looked slightly confused and anxious, and asked Janet if he could "have a few minutes." Glancing at her watch with more than a little irritation, Janet said, "Sure, Brandon, what's up?" Brandon began a loud, rambling monologue, sometimes making sudden gestures to emphasize a point. The general thrust of his concern seemed to be a movie that had upset him recently. The class had been shown a PBS film on "The Armenian Genocide," and Brandon had been moved by it. "But," he said, "I'm really pissed off! I mean, it's not enough just to say that there was genocide. You have to do something about it! These people were just slaughtered! They were attacked for no good reason! It's just not fair. We have to fight back and we have to fight back hard!"

Janet was puzzled by this outburst, which was atypical of Brandon, and asked the young man if his background was Armenian (his last name was actually Irish). "No," he replied, "my family is Irish and Scottish. But that's not the point! Nobody should be bullied the way the Armenians were!" Janet was feeling increasingly annoyed by this late-afternoon tirade, and decided she needed to set some limits. "OK, Brandon," she said, "I hear you. What happened to the Armenians was very unfair, and the film was upsetting. Why don't you do a research paper on the topic? Maybe contact some Armenian advocacy groups and see what they have to say. Then we can discuss it."

Brandon shrugged and said, "Yeah, great. That's a really good idea. Thanks." Then, abruptly, and without making eye contact, Brandon stormed out of the classroom. Janet was perplexed but did not make too much of the incident. She had nearly forgotten about the episode until three days later, when she received a call at home from the school principal: Brandon had just been arrested for stabbing another student—an individual known as a bully and "gay basher" around the school. Janet later learned that Austin, the student who had been stabbed, had been baiting Brandon lately about "being queer." Apparently, unbeknownst to Janet, Austin had left a note in Brandon's locker a few weeks ago saying, "Fags don't live long!" Brandon, however, had not reported this to anyone at the time.

As Borowitz and Schwartz point out, "Few things make us feel so understood as when people open up to us and hear the full dimensions of all we are trying to express" (Borowitz and Schwartz 1999, 206). Conversely, Brandon's case illustrates that there are few things more frustrating and dispiriting that being superficially "listened to," or worse, ignored. As we shall see later in this chapter, the philosopher Martin Buber helped illuminate the difference between "surface listening and genuine attention" (Borowitz and Schwartz 1999, 206). In my own field of psychiatry, we often use an expression coined by psychoanalyst Theodore Reik, "listening with the third ear." As therapist James E. Miller explains, "Listening with your third ear is never an attempt to psychoanalyze someone, nor is it an effort to come up with a solution for another's problem. It is simply your openness to be sensitive to those messages that *may not have been uttered but have been nonetheless sent.*" (Miller 2003, 24, italics added).

We can all understand how Janet—overworked, overtired, and underpaid!—could easily have missed the underlying issue Brandon was desperately trying to communicate. Ideally, she might have said something like, "Brandon, you seem really upset about this movie—more than anyone else in the class who watched it. And you sound kind of angry, too. I'm a little worried that you're dealing with some problems you are not talking about. Is there anything besides the movie that's bothering you, and that you'd like to tell me about?" Now, a good psychotherapist would have said something like that, but it's not in all of our power to be a cross between Dr. Phil and Sigmund Freud. However, it *is* in our power to *listen attentively*, as the Talmud says, and to be a mensch when someone comes to us in obvious distress. And—while it is certainly important that a student "listen with open ears and open heart" to the teacher—the same may be said of the teacher's responsibility to the student. As we are told by Maimonides: "A man should take an interest in his pupils and love them, for they are his spiritual children who will bring him happiness in this world and in the world hereafter" (Mishneh Torah 4; cited in Minkin 1987, 290).

Barry had been going through a "rough patch" in his marriage, and he hoped that a dinner with his brother Joel might help him feel a little better.

Although Barry and Joel lived in different parts of the state and had drifted apart a bit over the years, they had kept in touch with each other via telephone and email. Over a nice Italian dinner and several glasses of wine, Barry felt comfortable talking about the problems he and his wife Dorrie had been having lately. Unfortunately, Joel was not in the most receptive or attentive mood. When he wasn't interrupting Barry, he was diminishing Barry's misfortunes with comments like, "You think you have it rough! Let me tell you a little about what I go through with Janet!"

Joel was also experiencing financial problems with his home internet business, and talked at great length about "lost accounts," "cut-throat competition," and "the damn IRS." Joel confessed that he and Janet faced possible foreclosure on their mortgage. As he consumed more and more wine, Joel became increasingly loud and vituperative, at one point telling Barry, "Listen, boychik, you shouldn't complain about Dorrie! At least you have a decent job and a roof over your head!"

Simeon ben Zemah Duran (1361–1444), a Spanish rabbi and commentator on Pirke Avot, noted that, *"man has two ears but only one tongue, suggesting that his speech ought to be little and his hearing much"* (cited in Golden 1957, 75). No doubt, Barry would find this a compelling maxim, after enduring his brother's boorish and self-involved behavior! (Of course, given Joel's own problems, we may want to "cut him some slack" in this instance.)

The Rabbis regarded attentive listening as an essential quality for learning Torah, and there is no disputing that point. But in broader terms, *attentive listening is critical for all mature and caring relationships*—and it is a cardinal virtue in the mensch. Empathic listening, however, is no easy task. As Rabbi Dovid Rosenfeld tells us,

> Listening is not an inborn talent—and most of us are not very good at it. We listen to others with half an ear while being preoccupied with our own problems and affairs. We usually have to force ourselves out of our own little worlds to open up to what others are saying to us—to recognize that someone else's "world" is as important as our own. Our relationships suffer, but it is not very often that we overcome our natural self-centeredness to give others the attention they deserve" (Rosenfeld 2008).

Finally, commenting on Rabbi Akiva's statement that *"a fence for wisdom is silence"* (Pirke Avot 3:17), Rabbi Reuven Bulka observes, "to acquire wisdom, one should be silent or contemplative...rather than...eager to challenge" (Bulka 1993, 125). This prescription applies not only to students' behavior toward their teachers, but to anyone—like Joel—when listening to another human being's troubles.

PERSONAL ENCOUNTER—MARTIN BUBER AND A MISSED OPPORTUNITY FOR ATTENTIVE LISTENING

Rabbi Telushkin relates a story concerning the great Hasidic philosopher and scholar, Martin Buber (1878–1965), to whom we referred earlier. Buber was a controversial figure in Judaism, warmly embraced by those of a humanistic-liberal bent, but sometimes sternly criticized by Orthodox Jews (Levenson 2000, 88). Buber is best known for his classic work, *I and Thou* (1923), in which he distinguished two archetypal relationships: "I-Thou" relations, in which one person views another as a full-fledged human being, worthy of respect, understanding, and empathy; and "I-It" relations, in which one person treats another as a kind of useful object. Unfortunately, we often treat others as mere agents of our own needs—in effect, as walking utensils—and relate to them in an "I-It" fashion:

> Rather than truly making ourselves completely available to them, understanding them, sharing totally with them, really talking with them, we observe them or keep part of ourselves outside the moment of relationship. We do so either to protect our vulnerabilities or to get them to respond in some preconceived way, to get something from them (Jewish Virtual Library 2010b).

Tragically, on one occasion, Buber was unable to realize the very sort of "I-Thou" relationship he championed. It seems that Buber was hard at work editing a mystical text when his doorbell rang. A very distraught young man asked Buber if he could speak with him. Impatient to return to his scholarly work, Buber somewhat reluctantly agreed to hear the man out. Buber answered the questions the young man asked, but, as Buber later confided, "I didn't try to answer the questions he didn't ask." A short time later, Buber learned that the young man had apparently killed himself. As Telushkin reminds us, "when somebody seeks you out…listen. While he or she is speaking, stay focused; don't let your mind wander to other subjects, or to personal concerns. Listen—*really* listen." (Telushkin 2000, 407). And, as we say in my profession, "Try to listen with the third ear."

Chapter Eleven

Acquiring Knowledge and Wisdom

An unlearned person cannot be scrupulously pious.

—Pirke Avot 2:6; cited in Zlotowitz 1989, 17

When a person is brought into the heavenly Court of Judgment, he is asked...Did you set aside fixed times for Torah study?

—Babylonian Talmud, Shabbat 31a; in ibn Chaviv 1999, 81

If you lack knowledge, what have you acquired? If you acquire knowledge, what do you lack?

—Numbers Rabbah 19.3; cited in Borowitz and Schwartz 1999, 11

A sage ranks higher than a prophet.

—Bava Batra 12a; cited in Elkins 2007, 130

Two of the 48 traits for acquiring Torah: "intuitive understanding [and] discernment."

—Pirke Avot 6:6; in Lieber 1995, 413

Rabbi Chanina the son of Dosa says: One in whom the fear of sin comes before wisdom, that person's wisdom endures. But one in whom wisdom comes before the fear of sin, that person's wisdom does not endure.

—Pirke Avot 3:11

He (Rabbi Chanina the son of Dosa) used to say: One whose deeds exceed the person's wisdom, that person's wisdom endures. But one whose wisdom exceeds the person's deeds, that person's wisdom does not endure.

—Pirke Avot 3:12

A Yiddish saying holds that, "As long as you live, you study." But as Borowitz and Schwartz suggest, the saying is easily transformed in the hearts of most Jews, to become, "As long as you study, you live" (Borowitz and Schwartz 1999, 254). Study—meaning, in the first place, *study of Torah*—is arguably one of the foundation stones of Jewish culture, ethics, and life. Without wisdom, Hillel teaches us, one cannot truly be holy (Pirke Avot 2:6). Furthermore, according to Elkins, "Neither priest nor prophet equals the importance of the scholar, the teacher, or the wise sage who masters the vast body of biblical and rabbinic literature and can interpret, explain and transmit that heritage to the next generation" (Elkins 2007, 131).

All Jews, Maimonides tells us—rich or poor, healthy or sick—are commanded to study Torah until the day of death. Indeed, in the rabbinical tradition, the concept of study is often mentioned in connection with *mortality*. Thus, in Pirke Avot 1:13, Hillel tells us that "one who does not study deserves to die." On first reading, this seems a bit harsh! Perhaps, as Rabbi Reuven Bulka suggests, Hillel meant to suggest that "one who consciously turns [one's] back on learning cuts the self off from meaningful living" (Bulka 1993, 41). Rabbi Shlomo Toperoff puts it more strongly: "if we neglect the study of Torah, we commit spiritual suicide" (Toperoff 1997, 55). Indeed, according to Jewish history and tradition, study is something quite literally "to die for." In the second century C.E., when the Romans in Palestine forbade Torah study on pain of death, Jewish sages and students gathered nonetheless, to study in secret. From this same period, we have the story of our "late blooming" Rabbi Akiba and his colleague, Rabbi Tarfon, hiding with their students in a farmer's loft, debating the question of which is greater—*study* or *practice*? We will return to this question later in this chapter.

Studying in Judaism is not for the sake of accumulating facts; rather, it is for the sake of *knowledge and wisdom*, which in turn lead us to *righteous action*:

> [N]o wisdom [in Judaism] is possible apart from respect for the person and goods of others. The element of knowledge is always secondary, in the wisdom literature, to that of action. To be wise is not so much to be able to comprehend the ultimate secrets of life as the ability to lead a good life….Character and learning are mutually dependent upon each other (Birnbaum 1964, 211).

Knowledge, in Jewish tradition, comes in many forms, and exists on many levels. In the Lubavitch or *Chabad* (*Habad*) tradition of Judaism—based on the philosophy of Rabbi Schneur Zalman of Liadi (1745–1812)—human intellectual powers are subdivided into three faculties, called *chochmah, binah,* and *da'at.* (The term *chabad* is an acrostic composed of these three elements). Each of these components has a rather complicated, spiritualized meaning

(Foxbrunner 1993), with the usual translations being wisdom, understanding, and knowledge, respectively (Leiberman 2008).

The Yiddish term *sechel* also appears frequently in Jewish writing, and conveys something a bit more down-to-earth than the three elements of *chabad*. As Rabbi Wayne Dosick cogently puts it,

> *Sechel* means much more than book learning, more than acquired knowledge. *Sechel* means deep understanding and insight; the ability to perceive and discern. *Sechel* means having common sense and "street smarts" — having the capacity to meet any challenge and to prevail through wisdom and wile (Dosick 1997, 94).

Although I may sometimes use the terms *"chochma"* and *"sechel"* interchangeably, Rabbi Dosick's definition of *sechel* is perhaps as close as we can come to what "knowledge and wisdom" really mean for the mensch.

In his *Guide to the Perplexed* (*Moreh Nevuchim*, often translated as *Guide for the Perplexed)* Maimonides viewed *knowledge of God* as the pinnacle and perfection of wisdom. But even such perfected knowledge carries with it an implicit call to moral action:

> Thus, perfection of the soul is reached through philosophical inquiry that brings a person to the knowledge of God and therefore to a knowledge of God's moral attributes...[which are] to be emulated. *Without this emulation, God is not really "known"* (Rosenak 2001, 255–6, italics added).

In short, the highest kind of knowledge lies in *emulating God's moral attributes*. Or, to put it in terms more congenial to the mensch, "the richest, most intricate wisdom of all is knowing how to live properly" (Borowitz and Schwartz 1999, 12).

Dr. Ralph Jacobs, an elderly family practitioner, had treated Paul and his family for more than thirty years. Dr. Jacobs had taken care of not only Paul and his wife, Selma, but also their two children. When Paul, at the age of 60, complained of depression, weight loss, and vague abdominal complaints, Dr. Jacobs carried out a thorough medical work-up. Unfortunately, the tests revealed that Paul had cancer of the pancreas, with clear evidence of spread (metastasis) to other organs. The chances of Paul's surviving more than a year were extremely low—probably under 25%. (Only about four percent of all patients are still alive five years after a diagnosis of pancreatic cancer). Furthermore, there were no treatment options that were likely to extend Paul's life by more than a month or two, at best. Dr. Jacobs had seen many patients with cancer over the years, but Paul's situation was particularly vexing for him. After all, Dr. Jacobs had been very close to Paul and his family, and the prospect of this untimely death was understandably upsetting. Then there was the difficult issue of what, precisely, to say to Paul about his diagnosis and prognosis. Ever since he had known Paul, Dr. Jacobs had sensed a certain orientation toward avoiding "bad news" on Paul's part. "When the 'Big D' comes for me," Paul had once confided to Dr. Jacobs, "I don't wanna know about it...I just want to go out and play golf!" When Selma had been gravely ill with a burst appendix a year ago, Paul's attitude was, "Doc, I trust you. Just take care of her. I don't want to know all the statistics." In the face of this grim news, Dr. Jacobs began searching for ways of presenting the situation to Paul and his family. He read several articles in the "medical ethics" literature, most of which advocated "fully informing the patient with a terminal illness of all the facts." He read several religiously-oriented views as well, even though Paul and his family did not identify strongly with any particular religion. Finally, Dr. Jacobs arranged to meet with Paul and Selma in their home, rather than in his office. He said the following. "Paul and Selma, I have the results back from Paul's tests. I'll go over them with you in as much detail as you want, Paul. But first, I would like to hear from each of you how I can be most helpful and what you'd really like to know." Selma spoke first, saying, "Ralph, we've known you a long time. I trust you to tell us what we need to know, and I'll go with Paul's best judgment." Paul looked very somber and reflective. Finally, he spoke. "Ralph," he said slowly, "I know something serious is going on. I can tell just by your face. And I can feel it inside me, too. I don't need to know all the details. Just tell me this: do I have a chance of beating this thing, and should I start getting my affairs in order?" Dr. Jacobs replied as follows: "Paul, you do have a chance of beating it. Everybody is different, and what applies on the average may not apply to you. What you have is very serious, though, as you suspect. It would be a wise thing to get your affairs in order, and if things should turn out for the better, then we'll all lift a glass of wine in thanks!" Eventually, Paul did ask Dr. Jacobs for the precise diagnosis, and was told of his cancer; however, Paul did not ask any more about his chances for survival. He did indicate that he did not want any "chemo" or other aggressive treatment. Paul managed to live another seven months, with relatively good quality of life for most of that time.

As Dr. Fred Rosner, an expert on Jewish medical ethics, has pointed out, "Bioethicists now favor full disclosure as a means of respecting patient autonomy" (Rosner 2004, 949). However, he goes on to say,

> The Jewish view toward full disclosure of a fatal illness to a patient and especially a patient who is terminally ill is in general a negative one because of the fear that the patient may give up hope, suffer severe mental anguish (*tiruf hadaat*), become

despondent, and die sooner than otherwise. Shortening a patient's life is strictly forbidden because Judaism espouses the concept that God given life is sacred, even only a short period thereof. Disclosure should be couched in the context of optimism. The most positive outlook should be imparted to the patient. Disclosure must be imparted with compassion, sensitivity and hope thus giving the patient an opportunity to "set his house in order" (Rosner 2004, 949).

A similar approach is also advocated by Rabbi J. David Bleich (in *Judaism and Healing*), as summarized by Rabbi Telushkin: i.e., "a patient should be instructed to take care of his affairs and make appropriate arrangements, but the patient also must be told that such advice should not be construed as an indication that death is near" (Telushkin 2000, 253).

Rabbi Elliot Dorff has pointed to the substantial risks inherent in concealing medical information from patients. His own work in hospice care has led him to conclude that,

> the vast majority of people who are seriously ill do much better if they are told the truth than if it is withheld from them, even for the benign purpose of keeping their spirits up. Patients know from their own bodies that things are not good. If everyone around them pretends that everything is fine when in fact it is not, patients will cease to trust anyone (Dorff 1995, 97).

Indeed, I agree with Rabbi Dorff, as a general matter. And yet, I also believe that our Dr. Jacobs demonstrated what we described earlier as *sechel*—the ability to "*perceive and discern*" beneath the surface of things. To be sure: Dr. Jacobs could have gone "by the book," which—in today's era of medical-legal liability and informed consent—probably would have led to his giving Paul all the medical "facts" of his situation. But this may not have done Paul any great kindness. In my view, Dr. Jacobs found his way to a deeper kind of knowledge and wisdom than that found in a journal of bioethics. *Knowing the quirks of Paul's personality*, Dr. Jacobs realized at a "gut" level that simply giving Paul the unadorned facts about pancreatic cancer would have left Paul in a state of *tiruf hadaat*—mental anguish. Instead, Dr. Jacobs opted for a gentler approach aimed at achieving *yishuv hadaat*—the Hebrew term for a calm, settled state of mind, or "equanimity" (Lew 2003, 170).

The late Rabbi Alan Lew (1944–2009) points out that "The word *yishuv* is a noun from the Hebrew root *yashav* meaning *to sit*" and that the concept of *yishuv hadaat* is closely linked with "sitting" (Lew 2003). In essence, wisdom sometimes resides not in ramming the truth down a distressed person's throat, but in simply "sitting" with the person. Sometimes, that is all a mensch should do. We implicitly follow this advice when we visit someone "sitting shiva" (i.e., honoring the seven day period of mourning): when we enter the mourner's home, we are instructed to *say nothing* at first, allowing the mourner to begin the conversation. The deep psychology beneath this custom respects the individual's emotional needs—for who knows what the mourner wants to talk about in times of such sorrow? As with psychologist Carl Rogers' "client-centered therapy," the idea beneath *yishuv hadaat* is to meet the person where he or she "is," emotionally speaking, rather than foisting our own agenda upon someone in distress.

In this regard, we briefly cite a tale from Rabbi Nachman of Bratslav. Rebbe Nachman (1772–1810) is a brilliant and controversial figure in Hasidic Judaism, perhaps best known for his spiritual "tales" (Steinsaltz 1993). One of Rebbe Nachman's most famous stories, as re-told by Rabbi Lew (2003), is about a Prince,

> who came to believe he was a turkey. He took off all his clothes and got under the table and lived there on scraps and crumbs and bones. The King called in many doctors, but none of them could cure him. Finally, he called in a certain wise man, who took off his own clothes and sat down under the table with him. I am a Turkey, the prince told him. "I am a turkey too," the wise man said. The two of them sat there together for a very long time and then the wise man said, "Do you think a turkey can't wear a shirt? You can wear a shirt and still be a turkey." So the prince put on a shirt. "Do you think you can't be a turkey and wear trousers?" So the prince put on his trousers too, and in this way, the wise man coaxed the prince to put on all his clothes, to eat real food, and finally to come up from under the table and to sit at the table, and in the end, the prince was completely cured.

Rabbi Lew goes on to cite Avraham Greenbaum, a contemporary Bratslaver teacher, who elaborates on Nachman's tale:

> The wise man went under the table, and the very first thing he did, his first lesson, was just to sit there. You might have thought he would have been anxious to get started and take the first steps in his plan to cure the prince. In fact, sitting was the first step. Indeed, if you think about the story as a whole, you notice that most of the time the wise man took to cure the prince was spent just sitting with him. This is because the ability to sit calmly is one of the most important prerequisites of *clear-headedness* (Lew 2003, italics added).

I believe this "clear-headedness" is closely related to what we mean by *sachel*, and what Pirke Avot means by the phrase, "intuitive understanding [and] discernment." (Pirke Avot 6:6). We shall say much more about this in Chapter 17, when we discuss the concept of *tact*—which is itself a profound kind of wisdom.

Finally, since we have been discussing healers and cures, there is one more point to be made about doctors and patients with life-threatening illnesses. According to a recent report (Wright et al. 2008), only one third of terminally ill cancer patients in a new, federally funded study said their doctors had discussed end-of-life care. Surprisingly, patients who had these talks were no more likely to become depressed than those who did not. Those who had "end-of-life" talks were less likely to spend their final days in hospitals, tethered to machines. They avoided costly, futile care. And their loved ones were more at peace after they died. However, *having an honest talk about "end-of-life" care is not synonymous with the annihilation of hope.* As the Lubavitcher rabbi (known as "Rebbe") Menachem Mendel Schneerson (1902–1994) has so eloquently written, "For all the authority that G-d has given a doctor, nowhere has a doctor been given the right to condemn a human being as incurable" (Schneerson 1995, 89).

Indeed, here is what the late Ronald M. Davis, former President of the American Medical Association said, regarding his diagnosis of pancreatic cancer—widely considered a "death sentence":

> As a physician, I know the survival statistics for someone with stage 4 pancreatic cancer. But if the five-year survival is 5 percent, that's not zero. And as someone with relative youth, good functional status, outstanding health care, love and support from family and friends, and a thirst for life that feeds into a strong mind-body connection, then who knows what the future holds for someone in my situation. So never take away someone's hope" (Davis 2008).

As a physician, I say, "Amen" to that.

Schuyler was considered the "resident genius" at a computer software firm that was known for its cadre of geniuses. At the age of 28, Schuyler had become one of the foremost developers of computerized market research methods in the country. Recently, USA Today *had run a piece entitled, "Boy Genius Cracks Computer Cookie Code, Tracks Your Online Choices." The piece described, in rather broad strokes, some of the methods used by Schuyler's company to track the tastes, purchases, and even web site "surfing" of its users. "It's all done using cookies," Schuyler explained. (In internet jargon, "cookies" are pieces of software that record information about you as you use the Internet). "What we do is perfectly legal. It's called 'data aggregation' and it allows us to serve our customers better by knowing some of their preferences." In truth, Schuyler had developed an ingenious method for combining an Internet user's personal information, buying habits, credit history, and even medical and educational information. By doing so, he was able to create a kind of virtual biography of any Internet user he wanted to "profile"—without, of course, obtaining the consent of the person being profiled. Schuyler's view was, "Hey, I'm not Mahatma Gandhi! My job is to make money for the company and out-perform the competition." His boss too was very supportive of Schuyler's work, which had "made the company a ton of money," as his boss put it. But then, on a whim, Schuyler turned his formidable data aggregation program loose on his fellow employees—unbeknownst to them—and created profiles on each of them. By sheer accident, Schuyler's boss discovered some of these profiles on Schuyler's computer (including a detailed and rather embarrassing profile of him!), and promptly fired Schuyler.*

At the beginning of this chapter, we quoted one version of mishnah 3:11 from Pirke Avot. Here is Rabbi Berel Wein's translation: "Rabbi Chanina ben Dosa says: Anyone whose fear of sin takes priority over his wisdom—his wisdom will endure; but anyone whose wisdom takes priority over his fear of sin, his wisdom will not endure" (Wein 2003, 119–21). No doubt, given all the brilliant thinkers in Talmudic times, there were many instances in which the Rabbis confronted individuals whose intellect outstripped their piety. So it is, too, in our own day, as the parable involving Schuyler shows. Rabbi Wein, whose commentary on Pirke Avot brings a modern perspective to this ancient text, elaborates on the problem:

> the products of wisdom, knowledge, and creativity cannot endure unless they are based on a sense of morality—on fear and avoidance of evil and sin. Only if built upon a moral foundation do wisdom and talent bear the stamp of eternity. An extreme but most telling example of this idea is the refusal of the world's medical community to use the medical research that Nazi doctors conducted... such research is morally stained (Wein 2003, xx).

Similarly, in mishnah 3:12 of Pirke Avot, we are taught that "Anyone whose good deeds exceed this wisdom, his wisdom will endure; but anyone whose wisdom exceeds his good deeds, his wisdom will not endure" (Wein 2003, 121). Elaborating on this, Rabbi Wein writes that

> [Acquiring] knowledge is not the fundamental basis of Judaism. Rather, the goal of Jewish life is human behavior. As I have pointed out before, many a great intellectual has been an awful person. The great rabbi of the Talmud, Rava, stated that "the goal of wisdom is repentance and good deeds, so that a person shall not study Torah and Mishnah and yet kick away his father and teacher" (Berachos 17a; Wein 2003, 121).

By exploiting unknowing others for personal and professional gain, Schuyler used his tremendous intellectual gifts without adequately considering the moral implications of his acts. This is not the way of the mensch!

PERSONAL ENCOUNTER: THE BESHT
AND "SOULFUL" WISDOM

As we have noted, acquiring wisdom is not merely a matter of gathering facts or engaging in study, in the rabbinic tradition. Wisdom is acquired through a process that integrates both emotion and reason. This, I would argue, is also the task of the mensch. He or she must be able to appreciate things logically, but must also must put "heart and soul" into life—not just brain!

In this regard, we have a Hassidic tale concerning the Baal Shem Tov (the "Besht") and Rabbi Dov Baer of Mezeritch. The Baal Shem Tov (translated as "Master of the Good Name") or Besht is the title given to Rabbi Yisroel ben Eliezer (1698–1760). The Besht is considered to be the founder of Hasidic Judaism, and a proponent of a mystical, supra-rational approach to Jewish worship and study. Rabbi Dov Baer of Mezeritch (ca. 1707–1772) was a scholar of great erudition, but was skeptical of the Besht's more intuitive and mystical approach. And yet, the two sages clearly respected each other. Once, while Rabbi Baer was visiting, the Besht challenged him to interpret a mystical passage from the Kabbala. Rabbi Baer dutifully interpreted the text. "I am afraid you really do not know anything," the Besht said. Rabbi Baer responded, "if you know a better way of explaining [the passage], please tell me." The Besht started explaining the passage, and the entire room filled with light. A burning flame surrounded the Besht, who said to Rabbi Dov Baer, "Your interpretation was the correct one, but your way of studying lacked soul" (Besserman 1994, 63).

Or, as the French philosopher Blaise Pascal famously put it, "The heart has its reasons of which reason is unaware."

Chapter Twelve

Caution and Prudence

I, Wisdom, live with Prudence...

—Proverbs, 8:12

A learned person...does not answer impetuously.

—Pirke Avot 5:9; in Zlotowitz 1989, 47

Avtalyon says, Scholars, be cautious with your words, for you may incur the penalty of exile...

—Pirke Avot 1:11; in Zlotowitz 1989, p.13

Rabbi Yishmael [son of Yose] said...one who is too self-confident in handing down legal decisions is a fool...[and therefore]...Do not act as a judge alone...

—Pirke Avot 4:9,10; in Zlotowitz 1989, 37

Rabbi Yehuda said, Be meticulous in study, for a careless misinterpretation is considered tantamount to willful transgression.

—Pirke Avot 4:16; in Zlotowitz 1989, 39

An accident is an accident when it could not have been anticipated. When it could have been anticipated, it is no accident [but rather, negligence].

—Rabbi Joseph Telushkin; Telushkin 2000, 369

The terms "caution" and "prudence" do not appear as frequently, in many lists of Jewish virtues, as do more foundational principles, such as kindness,

83

justice, charity, etc. This is in partial contrast to some of the classical Greco-Roman literature, in which *prudentia* [prudence] is enshrined as one of the four "cardinal virtues," alongside *temperance, fortitude,* and *justice*. Perhaps in one sense, prudence ought to be considered a foundational virtue, since without prudence, it is difficult to know how to *apply* virtues such as kindness or justice. Indeed, philosopher Andre Comte-Sponville argues that, "Without prudence, the other virtues are merely good intentions that pave the way to hell" (Comte-Sponville 1996, 31).

In truth, as the quotations above suggest, the Talmud is replete with references to *caution* or *prudence* of various types, particularly in relation to the responsibilities of scholars. For example, "deliberation" is one of the 48 traits required for the acquisition of Torah (Pirke Avot 6:6). Furthermore, the general requirement for caution in our every-day lives is implicit in several Talmudic teachings, and it is by no means restricted to scholars. This may be seen in some rabbinical rulings concerning *negligence*, which represents the *failure to exercise reasonable caution and prudence*.

Finally, the admonition to be *cautious with one's words* surely applies to politicians and statesmen, though sometimes one doubts that this concept has been sufficiently absorbed in political circles. Thus, when one world leader used the term "crusade" to describe America's efforts against terrorism, much of the Islamic world was outraged—feelings that reverberate to our detriment, even to this day. In this chapter, we'll apply some of these lessons to the responsibilities and qualities of the mensch.

Pete was a senior supervisor at a large child day-care center. A social worker by training, Pete was under enormous pressure to provide both direct service to children as well as administrative oversight of more than thirty employees. Each year, Pete had to complete an evaluation of each of his supervisees, based on their work performance, ability to work congenially with colleagues, use resources efficiently, etc. This year's evaluations were due in one week, and Pete had barely begun. To make matters worse, Pete had gotten some "scuttlebutt" about Pam, a new psychologist on the team, that reflected badly on her ability to get along with her co-workers. One document, from Pam's immediate supervisor, Jack, indicated that Pam "often ignores constructive suggestions from both co-workers and from this writer." Since he was rushing to complete his reports, Pete filled out the form for Pam with a notation that reflected Jack's claims, without doing any further investigation. When Pam received her copy of the report, she was furious. She demanded to speak with Pete, and asked, "Did you even think about talking to me first? Did you take the time to look into Jack's motives, like the fact that I rebuffed the sexual advances he was making?" Pete expressed his great em-

barrassment to Pam, and promised to re-write her evaluation. Unfortunately, the original report had already gone to Pete's own boss, at a higher level in the administrative hierarchy. A subsequent investigation failed to turn up any evidence that Pam had ignored "constructive suggestions" from Jack or any other co-worker.

Pete failed not only to exercise caution with his words, but also to consult adequately with others ("one who is too self-confident in handing down legal decisions is a fool...[and therefore]...Do not act as a judge alone..." [Pirke Avot 4:9,10]). Had he first met with Pam and Jack, carefully weighing and investigating what each had to say, Pete might have been able to sort out the truth and avert a major transgression—that of *motzi shem ra*. This Hebrew term is usually translated as "giving another a bad name" (Telushkin 2000, 64) and encompasses what we would classify as *libel* and *slander* (knowingly making false and defamatory claims). *Motzi shem ra* constitutes "the most grievous violation of the Jewish laws of ethical speech" (Telushkin 2000, 64). To make matters worse, Pete failed to abide by another important Talmudic teaching: "Judge all individuals charitably" (Pirke Avot 1:6). In effect, he *assumed the worst* about Pam without making even a token effort to establish the truth. (One might argue that, technically, Pete did not *knowingly* defame Pam, if he credulously and naively believed Jack's unsubstantiated claims. But whereas this might spare Pete the charge of *libel* under American law, it would not spare him the charge of *motzi shem ra*).

In the next chapter on "Discussing and Evaluating Others Fairly," we will explore the distinction between *motzi shem ra* and its disreputable cousins, *rechilus* (harmful gossip) and *lashon hara* ("evil tongue") (Finkelman and Berkowitz 1995, 284). Clearly, caution and prudence are the building blocks for the fair discussion and evaluation of others.

Brigid and Dan seemed to live a charmed life: she a successful real estate agent, and he an up-and-coming architect. They lived in a large and rather posh four-bedroom house in an affluent suburb, and they had just installed a large swimming pool in their back yard. However, since they did not have children, Brigid and Dan did not install a fence around the pool, feeling that "The odds anybody would get past the fence in our back yard are close to zero." One day, when Brigid returned home from work, she saw the neighbor's cocker spaniel literally "dog paddling" in the pool, apparently unable to get out of the water. She quickly helped the dog out of the pool and brought him back over to her neighbor's yard. Brigid mentioned the incident to Dan, who found it quite amusing. "Little varmint must have sneaked under our fence!" he said, shrugging the whole thing off. A month later, however, on a

Saturday afternoon, Dan heard a scream from the back yard. He ran out to discover the neighbor's three-year-old son flailing in the pool, struggling to stay afloat. Fortunately, Dan was able to save the child before any serious injury occurred; however, the boy's parents were furious that the pool was not "child-safe" and threatened to "sue for psychological damages." Dan and Brigid managed to mollify the parents with an assurance that a fence would be installed immediately.

As Rabbi Telushkin notes, "Biblical law distinguishes between accidents that a person couldn't have anticipated, and injuries resulting from negligence" (Telushkin 2000, 368–9). For example, if one chooses to keep a pit bull as a pet, and knows that the dog has a history of menacing the neighbors, the owner bears "moral and legal responsibility for any future injuries the animal inflicts" (Telushkin 2000, 368–9). In the events surrounding Brigid and Dan, there was clearly reason to believe that their swimming pool was a potential hazard—the cocker spaniel incident should have given them fair warning that their back yard fence was not adequate to prevent someone from falling into the pool. Yet despite this knowledge, they did nothing either to repair the existing fence (evidently, it was easy for a small animal to penetrate) or to fence in the pool. They were fortunate that the neighbor's child didn't drown. Dan and Brigid failed to exercise caution or prudence, and were guilty of negligence. *This is not something a mensch would have allowed to happen!* Of course, as Telushkin points out, not every accident constitutes negligence, and "just because there's a victim doesn't mean there's a villain" (Telushkin 2000, 368).

Roy was delighted that he was able to take his family on a long-awaited trip to the Caribbean. He had "heard good things" about the particular island and therefore had done very little research into the environs surrounding the family's hotel. One night, when the family had settled into their hotel room, Roy complained of "feeling restless." He told his wife, Linda, that he was "going for a short walk into town." Although Linda expressed some reservations about the neighborhood, Roy dismissed this by saying, "Oh, stop being a mother hen! I'll be back in no time." Roy walked about fifteen minutes from the hotel into the outskirts of town. Although the neighborhood looked quite seedy, Roy was attracted to the numerous coffee stands, restaurants, and night clubs. While stopping at a newsstand to look at a magazine, two men accosted him. One distracted Roy with a question in English, while the other grabbed his wallet, knocking Roy to the ground. Fortunately, he was not seriously injured.

The translator and physician Judah ben Saul ibn Tibbon (1120–1190) is credited with the saying, "*Be not like the bird that sees the seed, but not the trap*" (Gross and Gross 1992, 21). In the foregoing vignette, Roy clearly saw the seed but ignored the seediness! In the Talmud, we are taught in the name of Rabbi Chanina ben Chanina, "One who stays awake at night or who travels alone on the road, and turns his heart to idleness—indeed, he bears guilt for his soul." (Pirke Avot 3:5; in Wein 2003, 111). As Rabbi Berel Wein points out, Rabbi Chanina was essentially cautioning against wasting one's time—time that could be spent in Torah study. But we can also read in Rabbi Chanina's words an admonishment to avoid *needlessly* placing oneself in potential danger ("alone on the road"), especially *without making any attempt to understand the risks*. Roy's frivolous wandering into the town at night without having investigated the potential for robbery, muggings, etc., represented a failure to exercise due caution and prudence. Roy not only exposed himself to danger, he put his family's welfare in jeopardy as well. After all, if Roy had been stabbed or (God forbid!) killed, how would his family have felt? There is, indeed, an element of *selfishness* that inheres in such foolish or risky behavior, since uninformed risk-taking puts those we love in peril, too.

Ironically, for all his caution, Rabbi Chanina was martyred by the Romans—along with Rabbi Akiva—after the abortive revolt of Bar Kochba in the 2nd century C.E. But this was a time when "thousands of Torah scholars were hunted down by the Roman police" (Wein 2003, 112), and Rabbi Chanina no doubt felt that the risks of expressing his faith were worth the dangers. This is quite a different matter than taking a casual and heedless walk through a dangerous neighborhood!

PERSONAL ENCOUNTER: RABBI MENACHEM MENDEL SCHNEERSON AND A CASE OF PATERNAL NEGLIGENCE

Known simply as "the Rebbe," Rabbi Menachem Mendel Schneerson (1902–94) was head of the Lubavitcher movement for 44 years. The Rebbe is squarely within the Jewish mystical tradition. Indeed, according to the summaries of the Rebbe's talks provided by Rabbi Simon Jacobson, the Rebbe emphasized that, "to begin to understand G-d...we must learn to go beyond our own mind, our own ego, our own tools of perception" (Schneerson 1995, 214). And yet, the Rebbe also draws on traditional sources of Jewish "rationalism" and studied mathematics and science at the University of Berlin and the Sorbonne. In one parable told by the Rebbe, we see his commitment to caution, attentiveness, and fulfillment of our responsibilities to others:

> One night, when a rabbi was deeply engrossed in his studies, his youngest child fell out of his cradle. Even though the rabbi was only in the next room, he heard nothing. But the rabbi's father, who was also studying in his room upstairs, heard the baby crying. He came downstairs, put the baby back in the cradle, and rocked him to sleep. The [younger] rabbi remained oblivious throughout it all. Later, the older man admonished his son: "No matter how lofty your pursuits, you must never fail to hear the cry of a child" (Schneerson 1995, 157).

One might say that the difference between a *luftkopf* (roughly, someone with his "head in the clouds") and a *mensch* is that the mensch hears the baby crying and checks to make sure everything is alright!

Chapter Thirteen

Discussing and Criticizing Others Fairly

Rabbi Samuel ben Nahman admonishes: "Why is the evil tongue [lashon hara] called the thrice-slaying tongue? Because it slays the person saying it, the hearer, and the person spoken about."

> —Arachin 15b; cited in Borowitz and Schwartz 1999, 242

Rabbi Chana ben Chanina asks, "How shall we interpret the verse, 'Life and death are in the hand of the tongue' [Proverbs 18:21]? ...it means... that a tongue can kill as surely as a hand. But while a hand can only kill what is nearby, a tongue can kill everywhere its message goes.

> —Arachin 15b; cited in Borowitz and Schwartz 1999, 242

Rabbi Sheshet said in the name of Rabi Elazar ben Azariah, "If someone spreads malicious gossip against his neighbor, or listens to and accepts malicious gossip, or if someone gives false testimony about his neighbor, he deserves to be thrown to the dogs."

> —Pesachim 118a; cited in ibn Chaviv 1999, 177

All who descend to Gehenna [Hell] will come up except three...one who sleeps with a married woman; one who shames his friend in public; and one who calls his friend by a cruel nickname.

> —Bava Metzia 58b; cited in Telushkin 2000, 471

Rabbi Elazar ben Azariah said: I wonder if there is anyone in this generation who knows how to reprove [without embarrassing the other person (Rashi)].

> —Arachin 16b; cited in ibn Chaviv 1999, 783

The way we speak—and how we speak about others—is a central concern of rabbinical Judaism. Rabbi Yisrael Meir Kagan of Radin (1838–1933), known as the "Chofetz Chaim" (Seeker of Life), is usually regarded as the foremost Jewish authority on the rules of proper speech. His masterwork, *Sefer Shmiras Haloshon*—the book of "guarding of the tongue"—sets forth in minute detail all the ways in which we must avoid *lashon hara* and *rechilus* (Finkelman and Berkowitz 1995). As we implied in the previous chapter, these terms are closely related but subtly different. In the strict sense, *lashon hara* ("evil tongue") refers to any *true* statement that "lowers the status of the person about whom it is said" (Telushkin 2000, 64). So, if Jones is in fact a lazy person and you say to someone, "Jones is a lazy person," you have engaged in *lashon hara*. (If Jones were in fact *very industrious* and you had made this same statement, you would, technically, be guilty of *motzi shem ra*, or "giving another a bad name"). Talk that borders on *lashon hara*—termed *avak lashon hara* ("dust of the evil tongue")—is also prohibited. This is talk that hints at something negative about a person, but doesn't actually say it. For example, if you were to say to a friend, "Who would have guessed that Izzy would come so far in life, given all his difficulties?" you would be speaking *avak lashon hara* (Finkelman and Berkowitz 1995, 114).

Rechilus is sometimes translated as "carrying tales" (Twerski 2006), in the way that a peddler carries his wares from place to place. The Chofetz Chaim's definition of *rechilus* is somewhat more technical and detailed: it is "information that potentially can cause ill will [between Jews]" (Finkelman and Berkowitz 1995, 284). In essence, *rechilus* is *potentially harmful gossip*—which may nevertheless reflect reality.

Not all *rechilus* necessarily represents *lashon hara*. For example, you might say, "Wow, I understand Joe just spent $60,000 on a new Porsche!" and thereby engage in "potentially harmful gossip." Joe's neighbor, for example, might become jealous or resentful, even though the revelation about the Porshe *doesn't lower Joe's status or standing* (as lashon hara does). On the other hand, one might argue that all instances of *lashon hara* (status-lowering but correct claims) represent *rechilus* (information that may lead to ill will between persons). That is to say, it is hard to think of an example of *lashon hara* that lacks the potential to cause animosity or ill will (Finkelman and Berkowitz 1995).

In contrast to both these terms, *motzi shem ra* represents information that is *both derogatory and false*. One way of distinguishing *motzi shem ra* from *rechilus* is nicely illustrated by Rabbi Israel Salanter, cited by M. Hudson (1998): in essence, if you say that the rabbi is not much of a singer, and the cantor, not much of a scholar, you may simply be mouthing *rechilus*. But if you say that the rabbi is no scholar and the cantor is no singer, you are guilty of "murdering a good name" (*motzi shem ra*)! We will try to clarify some of these distinctions in our first vignette.

The rabbinical strictures against both *lashon hara* and *rechilus* are numerous. We are admonished, for example, to avoid exposing ourselves to malicious gossip, and to do our best to turn aside such talk as politely as possible. And yet, the Chofetz Chaim recognized that, in certain circumstances, the need for "attentive listening" may trump our obligation to avoid *lashon hara*. Thus, we are told that,

> There are times when *halacha* [Jewish law] permits listening to negative information which is of no relevance to the listener...Where the speaker feels the need to express his anger or frustration for relief of emotional pain, one is doing an act of *chesed* (kindness) by hearing the person out and expressing understanding of his feelings (Finkelman and Berkowitz 1995, 252).

This would apply, for example, to a therapist listening to the angry diatribe of a distraught patient, or to a spouse trying to lend a supportive ear to his or her mate. Thus, "when a husband or wife is in need of emotional support in dealing with difficulty... listening under such circumstances is constructive and is clearly permissible" even when the spouse is voicing harsh criticism of someone (Finkelman and Berkowitz 1995, 254).

But "attentive listening" must not cross a certain line: "While one must be prepared to hear out a spouse and offer emotional support when necessary, one must be ever vigilant not to be drawn into a conversation of *loshon hora* for no constructive purpose" (Finkelman and Berkowitz 1995, 254). Furthermore, the Chofetz Chaim adds that, "If the listener feels that the speaker can be made to understand how he misjudged the person responsible for his frustration, he is obligated to do so" (Finkelman and Berkowitz 1995, 252).

Greg was a junior partner at a small-town law firm that had four senior partners. When the senior partners met to consider which of the junior partners to promote, Bert, one of the lawyers, made a true but derogatory comment about Greg. Bert said, "Greg is a very smart young man, no question about that. But, to be frank, I think his sexual identity is a little, shall we say, fluid, if you get my drift." Indeed, Greg considered himself bisexual but never made a show of his sexual orientation and was, as another partner pointed out, "a paragon of discretion and good judgment." However, once Bert had raised his concern, the other partners balked at making Greg a senior partner. Greg, of course, was crushed by the decision but did not protest or cry foul in any way.

A few days after the senior partners had met, one of them—Henry—sat down with Greg in the coffee shop, and said, "You know, Greg, I was really

rooting for you. Too bad Bert had to mouth off about, uh, you know—how
you swing both ways."

It seems clear that, in this unfortunate series of events, at least two commandments were violated. When Bert made his comment about Greg's sexual
orientation, he was engaging in a form of *lashon hara*. How? In our present
cultural climate, Bert's statement had the effect of *reducing Greg's stature, in
the eyes of the senior partners* (Telushkin 2000, 64). Furthermore, Bert spoke
lashon hara even though Greg may indeed be bisexual. The second violation
occurred when Henry gratuitously and needlessly "unmasked" Bert in front
of Greg. This could be considered a form of *rechilus*, since, in the formulation of the Chofetz Chaim, Henry's (admittedly accurate) revelation could
potentially cause ill will between Greg and Bert (Finkelman and Berkowitz
1995, 284).

On this point, the Chofetz Chaim teaches as follows:

> The prohibition against speaking *rechilus* is highly relevant when a committee
> meets to consider an individual for possible enrollment…or appointment…
> Whether or not the final outcome is in the person's favor, it is forbidden to
> divulge the identity of anyone who expressed an opinion against the person. It
> is wrong for a member of the committee to tell the candidate, "I was on your
> side but was outvoted by my colleagues" (Finkelman and Berkowitz 1995, 288).

Peg was a critical care nurse who always looked forward to the relief of
her 35–minute lunch break. One of the pleasures of lunch was sitting down
with Rick and Jan, two of her co-workers, and just "schmoozing." Usually
their conversation dealt with sports, politics, or—when things had not gone
well in the Intensive Care Unit (ICU)—their feelings about caring for very
sick or injured patients. But lately, Rick and Jan had started gossiping about
some of the other nurses in the ICU. "Did you hear about Ralph?" Rick said,
barely concealing his glee. "He got taken to the woodshed by the Chief last
week. Showed up at work looking like he had been out on a bender." Jan
chimed in, "I heard he was out on the town with Becky. You know, the two
have them have been doing a little "horizontal salsa" lately, if you catch my
meaning!" Peg felt very uncomfortable listening to this kind of scuttlebutt,
particularly since she was friends with Ralph and Becky, both of whom were
in her nursing school class. Peg did not want to sound "stuffy" or "preachy"
in front of Rick and Jan, but felt that she needed to signal her discomfort to
them in some way. Rather than criticize them for gossiping, Peg made it a
habit either to get up from the table—feigning the need for a napkin or some
salt—or to change the subject, whenever Rick or Jan made snide comments

about other staff. This worked for a few minutes, but soon, either Rick or Jan would usually resume gossiping.

This vignette focuses our attention on the passage in the Talmud that states, "If someone spreads malicious gossip against his neighbor, or listens to and accepts malicious gossip... he deserves to be thrown to the dogs" (Pesachim 118a; cited in ibn Chaviv 1999, 177. Given how rampant gossip is these days—not only in person, but over the Internet, on television, etc.—the penalty of being "thrown to the dogs" may seem a bit outdated. But there is nothing outdated in showing care and respect for the reputation of another human being, no matter how commonly this principle is violated. Few of us, after all, would appreciate being discussed in the disparaging terms Rick and Jan used. When such inappropriate conversation takes place at the dinner table—as a result, say, of the children's repeating derogatory information about their schoolmates—some religiously oriented parents may be able to follow the advice offered by Rabbi Abraham Twerski. He advocates cutting short such talk, and "explaining to your children that you are tempted to continue the discussion, but that such conversations are forbidden by God" (cited in Telushkin 2000, p.73).

But what about when the gossip—*rechilus* or *lashon hara*—comes from a workmate or friend? What about gossip that one overhears in social settings? How should the mensch handle such situations?

The Chofetz Chaim invokes the commandment, "You shall reprove your fellow" (Vayikra 19:17) as a foundational principle in dealing with gossipers. He tells us that "Generally speaking, one is required to interrupt and reprove the speaker of *loshon hora*, and do his best to ensure that he put a halt to his sinful speech" (Finkelman and Berkowitz 1995, 234). In our vignette, Peg tried to discourage the gossip from her workmates by discretely getting up and leaving the table, but to no lasting effect. It would seem, then, that Peg should have said something by way of rebuke to Rick and Jan. Certainly, it would have been reasonable for Peg to say something like, "You know what, you guys? I love our lunch-time schmoozing, and I know we are all under a lot of stress. It's tempting to talk a little trash at lunch. But I just feel a little uncomfortable when we start talking about the people we work with. Maybe we can agree to take that kind of talk off our agenda, OK?"

This brings us to the countervailing principle of *gentle reproof*, which was foreshadowed in the quotation at the beginning of this chapter: "Rabbi Elazar ben Azariah said: I wonder if there is anyone in this generation who knows how to reprove [without embarrassing the other person (Rashi)]" (Arachin 16b; cited in ibn Chaviv 1999, 783).

Indeed, the Chofetz Chaim is keenly aware of the responsibility to avoid shaming the speaker of *lashon hara*. He teaches that, "Reproof [*tochachah*] must be administered with respect and understanding, and should be done in private whenever possible" (in Finkelman and Berkowitz 1995, 234, citing Rashi's comment on Vayikra 19:17). Furthermore, there are times when even the Chofetz Chaim views rebuke of *lashon hara* as counter-productive. Thus, rebuke would not be wise when "the speaker would likely react by expressing yet greater negativity towards the person he was speaking about, as a way of defending his sinful talk" (Finkelman and Berkowitz 1995, 234). So, for example, if Peg anticipated that rebuking Rick or Jan would have resulted in their becoming defensive and even more vituperative, she would have been wise to avoid a confrontation. It may also be better not to reprove the speaker of *lashon hara* if one has good reason to believe that he or she is completely unaware that gossiping is morally wrong (Finkelman and Berkowitz 1995, 410)—and, in this day and age, perhaps there really are such individuals! Furthermore, the Chofetz Chaim advises that, "in an unreceptive group setting, it is wise to refrain from excessive reproof" (Finkelman and Berkowitz 1995, 236).

In short, when and how to deal with speakers of *lashon hara* is a matter of delicacy, judgment, and *tact*—a topic we will address in detail in Chapter 17.

Sarah and Bess had been good friends for more than thirty years. Sadly, now in their mid-thirties, both had been through painful separations and divorces. Both women were now, as Sarah put it with her usual sardonic humor, "Looking for Mr. Reasonably Goodbar." Within the past few months, Bess had been dating Tom, a successful engineer who had himself just come through a messy divorce. Bess had found Tom an intelligent, attractive and considerate person, and told Sarah, "This time might be the lucky charm." In the past week, Tom had actually suggested that he and Bess "move in together and really give this thing a chance." One day, however, Sarah was passing by her favorite restaurant and happened to spot Tom sitting and holding hands with a very young and attractive woman. Sarah felt a sinking feeling in her stomach as she debated what, if anything, to say to Bess.

The Talmud recognizes that some situations are morally ambiguous, as regards *lashon hara* and *rechilus*. And, there are also some instances in which informing a friend of a third party's apparent misbehavior would be morally wrong. For example, if Sarah had overheard one of Bess's workmates casually making a snide remark about Bess, it is unlikely that any great good would come of reporting the incident to Bess. This sort of speech would most likely fall under the rubric of *rechilus*—information which, while accurate, may lead to ill will between two people.

The situation might differ, however, if Bess were up for a promotion, and Sarah had overheard a workmate transmitting false and damaging information about Bess to Bess's boss, who was about to rule on the promotion. In that case, there might well be a legitimate good achieved by informing Bess of the workmate's malfeasance, since Bess might be able to correct her boss's mistaken impression and save her promotion.

We can use this line of reasoning to help answer the question of what Sarah should tell Bess regarding Tom, and his apparent infidelity. On the one hand, it is possible (if far-fetched) that the young woman holding hands with Tom was not his paramour, but, say, his 18–year-old daughter. On the other hand, if Tom is having an affair behind Bess's back and also urging that they move in together, real emotional harm could come to Bess if she remains unaware of Tom's deception and infidelity. As Bess's friend—and as a *mensch*— Sarah is obligated to let Bess know what she saw, without necessarily casting the events in the worst possible light. For example, Sarah might say, "Bess, I don't know what to make of this, and maybe there is an innocent explanation. But I feel I need to tell you that I saw Tom holding hands with a young woman in the restaurant today." This, too, would be painful for Bess to hear, but might prevent her from making a far more costly mistake. In the Chofetz Chaim's philosophy, these ideas are summarized as follows:

> People who speak *rechilus* usually have some motive in mind which they consider a positive one. The Torah's view, however, is that unless the motive is clearly constructive, the speaker is doing nothing more than gossip-mongering and his words are strictly forbidden. The most common constructive motive that would permit relating such information is to forewarn a person of someone else's intent to harm him, so that the person can protect himself; to inform a person that someone is *presently* harming him, so that he can put an end to the situation; or to tell a person that someone *has already* harmed him, so that he can seek restitution for the damage (if it is monetary) or at least prevent any further damage (Finkelman and Berkowitz 1995, 324).

In short, negative reports that are transmitted *l'toeles*—for a *constructive purpose*—may sometimes be permissible and even constitute a *mitzvah* (Finkelman and Berkowitz 1995, 322). The real mensch will take pains to make sure that he or she has all the relevant facts and is acting from a clearly beneficent motive, before passing along such information.

Finally, there is another class of speech that is forbidden in Judaism, known as "oppressive speech" (*ona'at devarim*). Oppressive speech may be of two types, as Rabbi Elliot Dorff explains (Dorff 2005, 86–89). The first type is speech that essentially wastes another's time and falsely elevates his hopes. For example, if you asked a merchant, "How much does this item cost?" when you had no intention whatsoever of purchasing it, you would be burdening the merchant with oppressive speech. The second type is speech that, in modern parlance, "lays a guilt trip" on somebody. So, if you were visiting a friend who had lung cancer, and said to him, "God, Irv, if only you hadn't *smoked* for the last thirty years!" you would be guilty of *ona'at devarim*. (In addition, you would have left Irv in a state of in a state of *tiruf hadaat*—mental anguish—which is inexcusable!)

We will say a good deal more about this second type of oppressive speech in our chapter on "Politeness and Tact" (Chapter 17).

PERSONAL ENCOUNTER: RABBI AHRON SOLOVEICHIK AND COUNTERACTING *LASHON HARA*

Known as "Rav Ahron," Rabbi Ahron Soloveichik (1917–2001) came from an illustrious rabbinical family. His father, Rav Moshe, was an esteemed rabbi, and his older brother, Rabbi Joseph B. Soloveichik, known simply as "the Rav," is considered one of the leading rabbinical scholars of our age. One anecdote concerning Rav Ahron tells how once, when the rabbi was a young man living in New York,

> he was waiting for the subway when a woman pushed him and herself [o]nto the tracks. A train was approaching, and he struggled to get not only himself out of harm's way, but her as well. So taken with his kindness was a nearby priest that he asked Rabbi Soloveichik to bless him on the spot (Dayan 2008).

Rav Ahron was regarded as a leading expert in *halakha*, Jewish law, and is cited by Rabbi Daniel Z. Feldman on the matter of counteracting gossip or *lashon hara* (Feldman 1999, 148). There are times, as Rabbi Feldman notes, when asking forgiveness (*mechilah*) may do more harm than good. For example, let's suppose you had spoken ill of your friend Joel in front of another friend, Mike. But suppose you knew that Mike had shrugged off the comment and had forgotten about it entirely by the next day. Should you go to Joel *now*, or perhaps weeks or months later, inform him of what you said in front of Mike, and ask his forgiveness? Or would that simply inflict unnecessary emotional pain on Joel for no good purpose?

Rav Ahron suggests that in circumstances like these, one might do better by dispersing information "that will counteract the negative effects of the gossip...such action is more consistent with increasing harmony than [is] seeking the victim's pardon" (Feldman 1999, 150). So, in effect, if you had said something to Mike along the lines of, "Joel is a bit stuck up," you might make amends by spreading the word that, "Joel is a person of great humility."

It is true, of course, that you can't "unring a bell." Nevertheless, we are reminded of the noble statement of Rav Abraham Isaac Kook: "The purely righteous do not complain about evil; rather, they add justice."

Chapter Fourteen

Honesty and Integrity

Rabban Shimon the son of Gamliel says: The world is preserved through three things: truth, justice, and peace...

—Pirke Avot 1:18

Stay far away from falsehood.

—Shemot [Exodus] 23:7

When a person is brought into the heavenly Court of Judgment, he is asked: "Did you deal honestly?"

—Shabbat 31a; in ibn Chaviv 1999, 81

Your "yes" should be honest, and your "no" should be honest.

—Baba Metzia 49a; in ibn Chaviv 1999, 527

A man is forbidden to make a habit of using smooth and deceptive language. There shall not be one thing in his mouth and another in his heart, but what is within shall be like what is without.

—Maimonides, Laws Concerning Character Traits 2:6; in Weiss and Butterworth 1975, 33

Great is peace, seeing that for its sake, even God modified the truth.

—Yevamot 65b

Along with peace and justice, truth (*emet*) is one of the pillars that supports the world's existence (Feldman 1999, 65). Rabbi Reuven Bulka observes that, "Truth is the basis of all social contact. If what one says is not what one means, suspicion and alienation will reign instead of trust and acceptance" (Bulka 1993, 48). Rabbi Feldman, citing the anonymous 14th century work, *Orchot Tzaddikim (Ways of the Righteous Ones)*, adds that, "It is not enough merely not to lie; rather, one must take extra action to ensure that one does not speak falsehood even inadvertently" (Feldman 1999, 70).

Furthermore, there is a close connection between speaking honestly and refusing to listen to malicious lies (*motzi shem ra*), discussed in the previous chapter. As Rabbi Eliezer Friedman notes, the commandment to "stay far away" (*tirchak*) from falsehood requires "avoiding being one who *hears* lies, not just avoiding being the one who tells them" (Feldman 1999, 68, italics added).

Nonetheless, the Torah does not necessarily take the view that *any* alteration of the truth—no matter how slight, and no matter the exigent circumstances—is absolutely wrong. Rather, the Torah "recommends that one 'stay away,' that is, strive to avoid a situation that will make falsehood necessary, even though, in such a situation, it then becomes tolerated" (Feldman 1999, 70). Indeed, we shall examine some situations in which falsehood of some degree may be permitted. Nevertheless, there is no denying that honesty is a foundational principle of rabbinical ethics—and a cardinal virtue of the mensch.

Roy had put in 20 years with his company, a small firm that specialized in printing mail-order catalogues for medical device companies. Roy worked as a clerk in the company post office, where he had access not only to regular stamps, but to the electronic stamping machine the company used to send out its correspondence. Over the past two decades, Roy felt he had been treated "pretty shabby" by the company. Despite his years of service, he had been turned down twice for a raise, and was even threatened with being laid off when he approached his boss about a two-week vacation—the only vacation time he had requested in twenty years. Meanwhile, Roy's family was struggling to cope with tough times, including paying for medical expenses stemming from his wife's dialysis. Roy decided to take matters into his own hands. He began pilfering small quantities of stamps from the office, which, as he put it, "didn't amount to more than a hundred bucks worth of postage" over a year's time. As his frustration and economic hardship grew, however, Roy clandestinely started using the company's electronic stamping machine for his own correspondence and packages.

It is not hard to understand Roy's frustration and bitterness. It may even strike some as "not a big deal" that Roy pilfered a hundred dollars' worth of postage, given what sounds like a callous and insensitive employer and the pressing needs of Roy's family. *And yet*: the Talmud takes a very clear and firm stance against such seemingly "minor" transgressions, particularly where one's business dealings are concerned. (By the way, a well-known U.S. Congressman was successfully prosecuted in the 1990s, as a result of his involvement in a conspiracy to launder Post Office money through stamps and postal vouchers.)

Regarding ethical conduct in business, Rabbi Joseph Telushkin observes,

> As the Rabbis understood God's will, a decent life...is defined first and foremost by being honest with others, particularly in monetary matters. If you cannot answer this question affirmatively...[*"Did you conduct your business affairs honestly?"*]... God is not going to be impressed with statements of faith and ritual observance (Telushkin 2000, 170).

The Rabbis of the Talmud were very specific as regards ethical business practices. For example, we are told, "The leveling rod may not be made thick on one side and thin on the other side" (Bava Batra 89b; in Katz and Schwartz 1997, 253). As Rabbis Katz and Schwartz explain,

> The leveling rod was an instrument used for measuring out quantities of grain...Apparently, there was a great deal of fraud going on in the buying and selling of grain, and the Rabbis were interested in setting up ethical business standards...A thin-sided rod would be...advantageous to the seller...[whereas] the thick-edged rod...would work to the buyer's advantage (Katz and Schwartz 1997, 253).

Accordingly, the Rabbis insisted that the rod be of two equal sides—thin or thick—depending on local custom. As we shall see in our "Personal Encounter" section, these matters of honest business practice greatly concerned Rabban Yohanan ben Zakkai. Clearly, they should have concerned Roy as well, and anyone who wishes to be counted a mensch.

Troy was convinced that he could close the deal. He had been trying to sell his house without using a real estate agent for nearly a year now, hoping to save the 6% realtor's commission. But in a very "soft" housing market, nothing had worked out as Troy had hoped. He had come down on the price four times in the past six months, and still, he had barely gotten any nibbles. Now, at last, he had a serious buyer. Glen and Heather were a recently married couple with a young daughter, and they were thrilled to find a house they liked. After having their own inspector check over the house, Glen and Heather were ready to say yes. First, though, Glen wanted information on *utility costs. "So, Troy, tell me, how much do you pay for gas and electric over the course of a year?" Glen asked. Troy hesitated for a second, then replied, "Oh, it never comes to more than $1200. And I can say that after ten years in the house." In fact, what Troy reported was absolutely correct—but he didn't tell Glen and Heather that he always spent winters in the Bahamas. Had he wintered in his New England home, Troy's yearly utility bill would easily have topped $2000.*

The Talmud tells us, in the name of Abbaye, "a person should not say one thing and think something else" (Baba Metzia 49a; in ibn Chaviv 1999, 527). Similarly, in his *Laws Concerning Character Traits*, Maimonides admonishes us that, "*A man is forbidden to make a habit of using smooth and deceptive language. There shall not be one thing in his mouth and another in his heart*" (cited in Weiss and Butterworth 1975, 33). Perhaps Troy was not in the habit of using deceptive language, but he certainly did so in his dealings with Glen and Heather.

Rambam provides us with another example of using "smooth and deceptive language." He writes, "[A person] shall not urge his friend to eat with him when he knows he will not eat, nor press refreshments upon him when he knows it will not be accepted" (Weiss and Butterworth 1975, 33). The dangers of such subterfuges were nicely brought home in an episode of "Curb Your Enthusiasm," in which the Talmudically challenged Larry David wants to avoid going to a friend's party. He cooks up the scheme of showing up at the friend's house the night *after* the party, bottle of wine in hand—assuming that this would signal his intention of coming to the party while allowing him and his wife to make a quick, apologetic exit. Instead, his friend invites Larry inside and regales him with boring stories, preventing Larry and his wife from fulfilling an important obligation that same evening. Bluffers, beware!

Maddy and Fred were newlyweds and had just moved into their new house. Fred was not on particularly good terms with Maddy's parents, who regarded him as "a little wet behind the ears" and not necessarily a reliable bread-winner for their beloved daughter. Indeed, Fred had suffered some setbacks recently in the start-up company he had founded, which was involved in testing various new technologies. Meanwhile, Maddy's parents had been "noodging" the young couple for months, angling for a chance to visit. Finally, the visit was arranged, and Maddy and Fred did their best to be gracious hosts. Their efforts, however, did not stop Maddy's mother Ruth from taking some pot shots at Fred. One night, in the kitchen, Ruth said to Maddy, "I don't see how you can buy a house like this, with a huge mortgage, and know that Fred is involved in this cockamamie company that will never make

a penny." Maddy defended Fred, but Ruth was unrelenting. "You should in-
sist that Fred get a real job with a real salary. Otherwise, you'll both wind up
in the poor house and your father and I will have to come bail you out." Later
that night, Fred asked Maddy what she and her mother had talked about. "I'll
bet she had some wonderful things to say about me," Fred said sarcastically.
Maddy said nothing, feeling under great pressure not to lie, but also not to
make matters worse between her mother and Fred. "Come on, honey, what
did your mom have to say about me?" Fred asked. "Well," Maddy replied,
"she said that she hoped your business would do well and that she wants the
best for us both."

So—was Maddy's response to Fred's question justified? Was it a bald-faced lie, or just a "little white lie"? The Talmud generally takes the view that, while honesty is surely the best policy, there are times when *absolute* honesty may not be the best response to the situation at hand. One way of stating this is to say that the truth may be "modified" for the sake of peace. One can imagine that "peace" here refers to the peace among nations, or the peace among family and friends. This attitude is based on a story in the Bible that involved Abraham and Sarah (Genesis 18:12–13), in which God actually "modifies" the facts concerning what Abraham's wife, Sarah, said about Abraham's age (Telushkin 2000, 102–3). Thus, "Great is peace, seeing that for its sake, even God modified the truth" (Yevamot 65b).

As Rabbi Telushkin puts it,

> When it comes to trying to reconcile feuding parties, Jewish law is remarkably tolerant of "white lies." Of Aaron, Moses' brother and Israel's first high priest, the Rabbis relate that he would utilize untruthful means to make peace between people who had fought. He would go to one, telling him how sad his adversary was about the dispute…then he would go to the other and tell him the same thing (Telushkin 2000, 103).

Judged on this basis, one can justify Maddy's "modification" of her mother's words about Fred. Indeed, it is the mark of a mensch to make careful judgments about how much truth is required to accomplish human and *humane* ends. One should employ just that much truth, but not necessarily more than that, *if the resultant harm of complete disclosure will outweigh the good.* Clearly, one needs to weigh such decisions carefully and honestly, and not concoct rationalizations for telling "little white lies" simply because it is *convenient* to do so.

Finally—though it may seem obvious in light of the foregoing—Judaism clearly permits telling a lie if doing so will save life or limb. Indeed, "Jewish law condemns as foolish and immoral both telling the truth to an evil person and thereby enabling him to go on doing evil; or telling the truth to an evil person that leads to your murder" (Telushkin 2000, 102). In short, "Truth is a high value; the saving of innocent life is a higher one" (Telushkin 2000, 102).

PERSONAL ENCOUNTER: RABBAN YOHANAN BEN ZAKKAI AND HONESTY IN BUSINESS

We mentioned Rabban Yohanan ben Zakkai at the beginning of this chapter, in our discussion of the "leveling rod," used to measure grain. Rabban Yohanan was deeply torn over whether to discuss the subtleties of the leveling rod in public. He said, "Woe to me if I speak, woe to me if I don't speak. If I speak, perhaps deceivers will learn; if I don't speak, perhaps the deceivers will say: 'The scholars are not experts in what we do!'" (Bava Batra 89b; in Katz and Schwartz 1997, 253).

In the end, Rabban Yohanan decided to discuss fraudulent measuring practices in public. His rationale was that the righteous will learn right from wrong, and the sinners—even if they are encouraged to deceive others—will ultimately stumble and be punished (Katz and Schwartz 1997, 253).

This same Rabban Yohanan, who lived in the first century of the common era (ca. 30–100 C.E.), was one of the primary contributors to the *Mishnah*, and a key figure during the Roman siege of Jerusalem (70 C.E.). Although a man of unimpeachable honesty and integrity, Rabban Yohanan did not hesitate to use a bit of trickery in the service of what he deemed a worthy cause. Legend has it that during the siege, Rabban Yohanan managed to escape by faking his own death and being carried out of the city in a coffin! This was not some self-serving dodge, however. Rabban Yohanan believed that negotiation with the Romans was essential, and he indeed managed to get himself to the camp of the Roman general (later to be Emperor), Vespasian. Apparently, and for unclear reasons, Rabban Yohanan did not try to persuade Vespasian to end the siege of Jerusalem. However, he evidently *did* persuade the Romans to spare the city of Jabneh, the main center of rabbinical scholarship (Bader 1988, 152–63). This could never have happened if Rabban Yohanan was not willing to practice a bit of deception!

Chapter Fifteen

Trustworthiness and Fidelity

When a man vows a vow to the Lord, or swears an oath to bind himself
by a pledge, he shall not break his word; he shall do according to all that
proceeds out of his mouth.

—Numbers 30:2

Rabbi Yehuda says: Better than...[making a vow and not fulfilling it, and
not making any vows at all] is making a vow and paying it.

—Chullin 2a; in ibn Chaviv 1999, 767

The business conduct of the disciples of the wise men is truthful and faithful. His "no" is no and his "yes" yes. He is scrupulous with himself in
his reckoning...He obligates himself in matters of buying and selling in
circumstances where the Torah does not obligate him, so that he stands by
his word and does not change it.

—Maimonides, Laws Concerning Character Traits, 5:13; in Weiss and
Butterworth 1983, 46

When [a person] makes a deal, he should not have in mind to back out of
it. But if he made a verbal agreement and retracts when the market price
changes, he is not guilty of breach of faith.

—Rashi, Baba Metzia 49a; in ibn Chaviv 1999, 527

One should not promise to give a child something and then not give it to
him, because as a result, the child will learn to lie.

—Sukkah 46b; cited in Telushkin 1994, 58

R. Yochanan said: If the Torah had not been given, we could have learned…not to engage in adultery from the dove [which is faithful to its mate].

—Eruvin 100b; in ibn Chaviv 1999, 152

The Hebrew term *emunah*—which is related to the word *amen*—is often translated as "faith." However, some scholars (e.g., Borowitz and Schwartz 1999, 27) translate it as "trustworthiness" or "faithfulness." Rabbi Dr. Isadore Epstein (1894–1962), the editor of the renowned Soncino Press Babylonian Talmud, explains why there is no contradiction between these views:

The Hebrew word *Emunah* has a two-fold connotation—theological and human. It signifies alike faith—trust—in God, and faithfulness—honesty, integrity—in human relations. These two concepts of *Emunah* do not conflict with each other; on the contrary, they complement and supplement each other. In Judaism, unlike other religions, faith is not some mystic quality charged with supernatural powers capable of winning divine favour and grace. Faith is a dynamic, a motive for faithfulness, and is of value only in so far as it is productive of faithful action; nor is there any faithful action that is not rooted in faith in God…For it is the man of the highest faith in God who is the man of the greatest faithfulness in his dealings with his fellow man; and it is only the man of faithfulness who can truly be considered a man of faith (Epstein 1948).

Those readers who are not necessarily believers in God—and, of course, one may be a *mensch* and still be an agnostic or an atheist!—may find Rabbi Epstein's argument a bit hard to grasp. Perhaps another way of understanding the kind of reciprocity Rabbi Epstein describes is to hypothesize something like this: if a person does not believe in *something larger than himself*, some higher concept of "the Good" to which one aspires, there is no morally compelling reason to keep one's word or honor one's promises. One has to "keep the faith"—that is, cleave to this set of supra-personal ideals—in order to remain faithful to others. Conversely, if one does not remain faithful to others—actually honoring one's commitments and keeping one's promises—then he or she breaks faith with, and even desecrates, that same set of transcendent values.

Note that "truthful" and "trustworthy" are closely related but somewhat distinct concepts, as are the terms *emet* (truth) and *emunah* (trustworthiness). A person who says he will pick you up for work each morning; fails to do so on two occasions; and then gives you absolutely honest explanations ("I forgot to set my alarm clock," "I was sleeping off a hangover," etc.) is certainly being *truthful*, but can't (in such circumstances) be called *trustworthy*.

Conversely, it is theoretically possible to imagine a person who is unfailingly trustworthy in fulfilling his obligations, but who is not especially truthful in many aspects of life. For example, a handy-man always shows up, right on schedule, to do the work you have hired him to do—but routinely lies to his wife about his drinking and spending habits. The ideal of the mensch, of course, is to combine *emet* and *emunah*. Maimonides seems to have something like this in mind when he writes that the disciple of the wise "is truthful *and* faithful" in his business dealings (*Laws Concerning Character Traits*, 5:13; cited in Weiss and Butterworth 1983, 46).

Larry was one of the few remaining owners of a "Mom and Pop" delicatessen and grocery store, located in a poor neighborhood outside Boston. Most of the other small, privately owned grocery stores in the region had been run into the ground by the huge, national chains that were able to sell food products for much less. Larry was able to stay afloat through a combination of his business savvy and his long-standing reputation for trustworthiness and flexibility. His catering service was especially popular in the neighborhood. Six months ago, Larry had worked out a special deal with his friend and long-time customer, Cal, who was planning a big college graduation party for his son. More than 150 guests were expected. To clinch the deal on the large catering order, Larry agreed, in writing, to give Cal a 10% discount on all meat prices. Unfortunately, Larry had failed to foresee the dramatic rise in the cost of livestock, stemming from the ethanol industry's strong demand for corn. The increasing cost of livestock had led, in turn, to a huge spike in the price of beef, pork, and chicken, nationwide. As Larry calculated it, the original deal he had worked out would end up costing him over two thousand dollars in lost revenues—a loss he could hardly afford. Larry felt that he should not be held to his original agreement with Cal, since he, Larry, "should not be expected to absorb costs that were totally beyond my control." But when Larry gingerly broached the issue of re-negotiating the deal, Cal became angry. "What kind of friend are you?" he shouted. "And what kind of businessman? I could take you to small claims court for this!"

So who is right in this matter? Maimonides teaches us that the righteous individual "*is scrupulous with himself in his reckoning...He obligates himself in matters of buying and selling in circumstances where the Torah does not obligate him, so that he stands by his word and does not change it*" (*Laws Concerning Character Traits*, 5:13; cited in Weiss and Butterworth 1983, 46). In this instance—one in which Larry agreed *in writing* to provide Cal the 10% discount—the Torah itself would have obligated him to keep his part of the bargain. As we are told, "*When a man...swears an oath to bind himself by a pledge, he shall not break his word; he shall do according to all that proceeds out of his mouth"* (Numbers 30:2). If this applies to a verbal agreement, it surely applies to a written one.

Had Larry made only a *verbal* offer to Cal, there might have been some disagreement among the Rabbis of the Talmud. There is an interesting exchange on this point in the Talmud (Baba Metzia, 49a*)*. Thus, "concerning a verbal transaction [where no deposit was given] Rav said, [If it is not carried out,] it does not involve breach of faith" (ibn Chaviv 1999, 527). But Rabbi Yose, son of Rabbi Yehudah, insists there *would* be a breach of faith, arguing that a verbal agreement must be kept. Abbaye weighs in by saying, "a person should not say one thing and think something else." At the end of this section, Rashi has the final word: "When [a person] makes a deal, he should not have in mind to back out of it. But if he made a verbal agreement and retracts when the market price changes, he is not guilty of breach of faith" (Rashi, Baba Metzia 49a; in ibn Chaviv 1999, 527).

To be sure, the "market price" changed in the case of Larry's agreement with Cal; but because their agreement was *in writing*, Larry would be obligated to keep his word. In this instance, Talmudic ethics would undoubtedly coincide with American contract law.

But wait—what about *Cal's* responsibility in this matter? Knowing the hardship the original deal would bring to Larry, who is, after all, a friend, does Cal have any obligation to re-negotiate the deal? Although this question is somewhat tangential to our discussion of "trustworthiness," it does raise an important concept in Talmudic ethics: namely, that of *lifnim meshurat hadin*, "going beyond the letter of the law" (Telushkin 2000, 289).

What does this mean? The one who goes "beyond the letter of the law" does not stand upon a strict legal principle, but instead, behaves like a *mensch*. Rabbi Telushkin gives this modern-day example:

> A window washer once came to a friend's apartment in Manhattan and, while preparing to clean a window, clumsily broke a valuable vase. Did my friend have the right to insist on repayment for its value? Yes, but he didn't. Did he have the right to deduct payment from the money he owed the man…? Yes, but he didn't (Telushkin 2000, 289).

So, although Cal certainly has the legal and even moral "right" to insist that Larry stick with their original contract, the principle of *lifnim meshurat hadin* dictates that Cal at least consider re-negotiating the terms, rather than ensuring financial hardship for a friend. For a more nuanced and detailed discussion of these issues, see Friedman and Weisel (2003).

Sandy had been dealing with her 10–year-old son Dylan's behavioral problems for more than a year, but with only limited success. Dylan was an impulsive boy with a great deal of "nervous energy." Sandy had been concerned enough to have Dylan evaluated for "hyperactivity," but a thorough neuropsychological evaluation had shown no evidence of attention-deficit hyperactivity disorder (ADHD). One of the problems Sandy faced was Dylan's refusal to "pick up after himself." Both Sandy and her husband Bob had made it clear to Dylan that he had to keep his room neat and not leave clothing all over the floor. When Dylan refused to abide by these rules, Sandy and Bob would impose various penalties, such as limiting Dylan's time playing with his electronic games. But punishment had only a temporary effect. Finally, Sandy decided to try "a different approach" and promised Dylan that if he kept his room clean for a month, she and Bob would take him to Sea World in Orlando—one of Dylan's most ardent wishes for years. But even as they made this offer, both Sandy and Bob knew in their hearts that such a trip would be very difficult, if not impossible, for them to make in the foreseeable future.

Lo and behold, Dylan managed to keep his room clean for an entire month. But when it came time for Sandy and Bob to follow through and keep their part of the bargain, they reneged. "Honey," Sandy said to Dylan, "I know we said we'd go to Orlando, but we just don't have the time right now—your Dad and I are just swamped with work." Dylan seemed to "shrug it off" at first, without any overt change in his behavior. He even continued to keep his room clean. However, a week later, Sandy got a call from Dylan's school principal, stating that Dylan had been caught stealing change from the class's UNICEF donation box. Worse still, Dylan had lied about it to his teacher, denying he had done anything wrong.

The Talmud warns us against making promises we cannot or will not keep, particularly promises made to a child: "One should not promise to give a child something and then not give it to him, because as a result, the child will learn to lie" (Sukkah 46b; cited in Telushkin 1994, 58). Indeed, as Shelley Kapnek Rosenberg observes,

> Our failure to honor such promises inadvertently teaches our children two troublesome lessons. First, we demonstrate that telling the truth and keeping promises are secondary to convenience or to a better offer. [In other words,] If it is inconvenient to keep a promise, it's okay to break it…Second, we indicate to our children that they are less important than our friends, business associates, or whoever took precedence over them…[Furthermore,] a pattern of broken promises may leave children feeling hurt, resentful, and devalued…children who feel devalued may devalue others, in turn. Moreover, these children may later find it difficult to build adult relationships based on truth and trust (Rosenberg 2003, 17).

Of course, consistency in "practicing what we preach" applies to many other behaviors besides making promises. As Rosenberg notes, "if we teach our children that they should not steal, then we should model that ideal in our own behavior" (Rosenberg 2003, 17–18). Moreover, the obligation to keep our promises extends beyond our children. When we break a promise to a friend or adult family member, we devalue that individual. In Martin Buber's terms, we turn him or her into an "It"—an object for our personal use and convenience—rather than a "Thou."

As Borowitz and Schwartz remind us (1999, 28), "How we fulfill our promises to those we love defines our basic trustworthiness. Jewish tradition teaches that we should not make oaths or vows or rash promises, but that our word and our promises must be our bond" (Reuben 2008).

Over the past month, Alex had developed an intense sexual preoccupation with Cortney, a woman about half his age, who worked in Alex's insurance office. Cortney was doing nothing to encourage Alex's attention and seemed oblivious to his constant preening and blushing in her presence. "I'm probably old enough to be her father," Alex told himself, feeling a sense of shame welling up inside. He had been married to Beth for over twenty years, and loved her dearly, despite Alex's feeling that "the spark has kind of died down lately." Alex had never been unfaithful, and he was certain Beth had never strayed from their marital vows, either. But over time, Alex's resistance to the idea of "a little fling" began to erode. "How much harm could it really do?" he began asking himself. "After all, most guys my age probably get a little bit on the side." One day, he approached Cortney and impulsively asked her if she would like to go out to dinner some time. To Alex's surprise, Cortney smiled and quickly accepted, adding, "I was wondering how long it would take you!"

This scenario is probably all too common in and outside the workplace. It seems there is even an Internet website that entices people with the teaser, "Life is too short, have an affair!" Yet marital infidelity (adultery) is strongly condemned in Judaism, and is understood as one of the most heinous forms of personal betrayal. The Talmud teaches us that even without the Torah, an observant individual would know that adultery is wrong, simply by observing the dove: "R. Yochanan said: If the Torah had not been given, we could have learned…not to engage in adultery from the dove [which is faithful to its mate]" (Eruvin 100b; in ibn Chaviv 1999, 152).

To be sure, the Talmudic tractate dealing with adultery (*Sotah*) speaks from a distressingly male-centered point of view: the term *sotah* means "a woman who has gone astray," and this tractate deals almost entirely with a *wife's* infidelity to her marital vows (Bokser 1989, 155–6). Rabbi Judith Hauptman deals with Tractate *Sotah* in detail in her book, *Rereading The*

Rabbis: A Woman's Voice. Hauptman takes the view that for all its "patriar-chal" inequities, *Sotah* also reflects the Rabbis' sincere attempt to treat wives with some degree of fairness, and to protect them from arbitrary and capricious prosecution at the hands of jealous husbands.

In any case, the Judaic tradition is clear in its condemnation of marital infidelity in general, and in its praise for *shalom bayit* ("peace in the family"). Thus, Rabbi Simeon ben Gamaliel teaches us that "one who brings jealousy and strife into his house" is like one who "had infected the whole House of Israel" (Avot de Rabbi Natan 28:3; cited in Rosenberg 2003, 85). And Borowitz and Schwartz note that, in the Jewish tradition, adultery constitutes treachery of such depth that we may be cut "too deeply for our love to survive" (Borowitz and Schwartz 1999, 35).

Rabbi Steven Carr Reuben describes the tremendous harm that comes from breaking faith with one we love:

> Betrayal leaves us heartbroken, afraid to trust, unable to feel safe enough to build lasting relationships. Judaism teaches that there are three levels of untrust-worthiness: deceit, hypocrisy and the worst of all, betrayal. We despise deceit and dissembling; hypocrisy fills us with revulsion. But being betrayed by one we love is soul destroying. We are only able to love, to feel ultimate trust when we feel secure enough to drop our innermost defenses, to expose our deeply defended vulnerabilities. The cry of "How could you?" is the cry of the soul's anguish when pierced in its primal core (Reuben 2008).

In contrast, Rabbi Reuben continues,

> When we are trustworthy we offer a firm foundation of support for others. We promise reliability, credibility and stability. We offer people hope. Being trustworthy means that we accept increased accountability for our actions as we mature. The greater our position of responsibility, the greater must be our own personal trustworthiness (Reuben 2008).

PERSONAL ENCOUNTER: RABBI SHIMON
RETURNS THE JEWEL

Rav (Rabbi) Shimon ben Shetach (ca.120–40 B.C.E.) was the head (*Nasi*) of the Sanhedrin, the Rabbinic high court, during a stormy period of Jewish history. During this time—more than a century before work on the *Mishnah* began—there was great strife between two sects or schools, known as the *Pharisees* and the *Sadducees* (Bader 1988, 72–78). While the ideologies of these sects need not concern us here, it is important to note that the Pharisees were really the progenitors of normative, "Rabbinical" Judaism, after the destruction of the Second Temple in 70 C.E. Rav Shimon was, at first, the only Pharisee in the Sanhedrin; but, by dint of argument and persistence, he was eventually able to replace the Sadducees with Pharisees (Bader 1988, 73). Rav Shimon was known for his very strict attitude toward enforcing the law. At the same time, he spent most of his life in poverty, and earned a livelihood as a flax merchant. Here is a tale told of Rav Shimon that clearly demonstrates both his integrity and his trustworthiness. The story is re-told by Rav Binny Freedman, as follows:

> It seems [Rabbi Shimon] bought a donkey from a non-Jewish fellow and was riding back to Jerusalem when one of his students found a rare and valuable gem in one of the saddlebags. Halfway to Jerusalem, Rabbi Shimon, without thinking twice, immediately turned the donkey around and headed back to find the original owner of the donkey. "But you bought the donkey with the saddle-bags!" exclaimed one of his students. "Isn't anything found in them rightfully yours?" "I paid for a donkey," replied Rabbi Shimon, "I did not pay for such a valuable gem." After [Rabbi Shimon returned]…the priceless gem to its original owner, the non-Jew, clearly overcome by Rabbi Shimon's integrity, exclaimed: "Blessed is the G-d of Rabbi Shimon ben Shetach!" (Freedman, n.d.).

Chapter Sixteen

Gratitude and Contentedness

Ben Zoma says: ...Who is rich? One who rejoices in one's portion...

—Pirke Avot 4:1

A good eye, a humble spirit, and a contented soul are the traits of the disciples of our father Avraham...

—Pirke Avot 5:22

Who seeks more than he needs, hinders himself from enjoying what he has. Seek what you need and give up what you need not. For in giving up what you don't need, you'll learn what you really do need.

—Solomon ibn Gabirol, Mivhar Hapeninim 155, 161; cited in Borowitz and Schwartz 1999, 164

Ben Zoma...customarily said: "What labors did Adam have to carry out before he obtained bread to eat? He plowed. He sowed. He reaped. He bound the sheaves, threshed the grain...I, on the other hand, get up and find that all these things have already been done for me."

—Berakhot 58a; cited in Dorff 2005, 102

What we would call "gratitude" and "contentedness" correspond roughly to the Hebrew terms, *hakarat hatov* and *histapkut,* respectively (Telushkin 2000, 92; Borowitz and Schwartz 1999, 161–72). Together, these states of mind and soul might be subsumed under the English term, *thankfulness.* Rabbi Toperoff points out that the mishnah cited above, regarding "Who is rich?" (Pirke Avot 4:1) is not fundamentally about being "rich," but about being *happy* or contented. Rabbi Toperoff cites the words of the 13th century sage, Jacob Anatoli, who said, "If a man cannot get what he wants, he ought to want what he can get" (Toperoff 1997, 197). This Talmudic notion of happiness, as Toperoff points out, stresses the "great attribute of thankfulness"—surely an essential character trait in the mensch.

Lori Palatnik (2000) has observed that, "Being a Jew is synonymous with expressing gratitude." Indeed, Jews are supposed to begin each day with a prayer of thankfulness, known as the *modeh ani*. In English, the prayer goes, "Thankful am I before you, living and eternal King, that you have returned my soul within me with compassion, abundant is Your faithfulness" (Rigler 2001). Note that the term "faithfulness" (*emunah*) appears here, in connection with thankfulness. In effect, we return God's faithfulness with our own, by expressing a prayer of thanksgiving each day.

Thankfulness is much more a matter of *perspective* than of possessions. The Stoic philosopher Seneca (4 B.C.E.-65 C.E.) put it this way: "It is in no man's power to have whatever he wants; but he has it in his power not to wish for what he hasn't got, and cheerfully make the most of the things that do come his way" (Letter CXXIII, in Campbell 1969, 227).

A more homely way of expressing this idea is nicely summarized in a Jewish folk tale, as told by Borowitz and Schwartz:

> Once a poor Hasid became so distraught because of the overcrowding in his hovel that he appealed to his Rebbe, "We have so many people living with us that we can't turn around in the house." The Rebbe counseled the man...[to move his goat, then his chickens, and then his cow] into the house. [The man] returned, half crazed, to the Rebbe. "It's the end of the world," cried the man. The Rebbe responded, "Now go home, turn out the goat, chickens and cow, and report to me tomorrow." The following day the Hasid showed up beaming. "Rebbe! My hut seems like a palace now!"'

Rick was known in the office as "one of the movers and shakers." At the age of only 32, Rick was already Vice President of Corporate Management in a large biotechnology firm. Rick's friends saw him as a man who "had it all"—good looks, a great career, a beautiful and successful wife (who worked as a photographer), and a gorgeous house. Yet almost nobody saw the Rick who left the office and went home at night, feeling like a "fraud" and a "flop." Rick castigated himself for "not making it to President of Corporate Management" and for "getting edged out by a guy with more guts." Rick looked at his twelve-room house in an exclusive suburb and thought, "I could have done better than this. There are guys at the company making the same as me who have a house twice the size of ours, with a pool and a Jacuzzi."

Even in his marriage, Rick always wished for more. "I love Kathy," he said, "and she is a wonderful wife, but in a lot of ways, she's not the woman

I dreamt of marrying. I always wanted a wife who loves to travel, and Kathy is kind of a stick in the mud. She just wants to stay home and work on her photography."

Rick is one of millions of Americans who just can't seem to find contentment, despite the many wonderful things (and people) in their lives (Pies 2008, 60–61). As Borowitz and Schwartz sadly note, citing the Yiddish proverb that *"Better has no limits"*:

> We are consumed with consuming...Thus people spend fortunes decorating their homes and then soon come down with cabin fever inside them....Give us the chance and we fill our walk-in closets until they overflow and then build additions to our homes to accommodate our still never-ending "stuff" (Borowitz and Schwartz 1999, 167).

Similarly, Rabbi Steven Carr Reuben observes that,

> no matter how much of anything we have, we could always use more—more money, more possessions, more love, more space, more time, more pleasure— and this fact is one of humanity's greatest sources of dissatisfaction, frustration, jealousy, and anger (Reuben 1997, 187).

There is a saying from a haggadic commentary on *Ecclesiastes*, to the effect that, "People never leave this world with even half their desires fulfilled" (Koheles (Ecclesiastes) Rabbah 1:13). If we truly understood this reality and lived out its implications, we would probably find the happiness that has eluded Rick.

Sarah and Walter were a married couple in their late 60s who lived along the banks of the Cedar River, near Cedar Falls, Iowa. In the spring of 2008, the Mississippi and Cedar Rivers overflowed their banks and breached several levees. Sarah and Walter's house was flooded, destroying all the furniture, carpets, and belongings on their first floor. The couple had scrimped and saved for nearly thirty years to buy and furnish their house, and had just paid off their mortgage. Like many in their area, they did not have flood insurance. Among the items lost were several photo albums of great sentimental value, along with Walter's prized stamp collection. At first, Sarah and Walter felt angry and bitter, as well as bereft. They complained that "nobody gave us enough warning" about the flooding, and that city officials had been slow to protect their property. But while staying with some friends in a neighboring town, Sarah and Walter learned of an elderly neighbor who had lost her entire house, as well as her two beloved dogs. Other families in the Midwest, they soon found out, had lost loved ones in the flooding. As their own friends and family rallied to help them recover, Sarah and Walter realized that they had many reasons to feel grateful.

Some individuals who survive disasters go on to be bitter and angry—cursing God, fate, the government, etc. To some degree, this is understandable; after all, we are accustomed to our usual possessions, our house, our livelihood, and so on, and when these things are suddenly taken from us, we may lash out at someone or something. But Sarah and Walter moved away from such feelings toward the realization that they had been spared much worse. The medieval poet and philosopher Solomon ibn Gabirol (ca. 1021–1058 C.E.) wrote that, *"in giving up what you don't need, you'll learn what you really do need"* (cited in Borowitz and Schwartz 1999, 164). What we truly *need* in the midst of disaster is our own bodily survival and the ability to keep a cool head. If we are fortunate, we may also be blessed with the love and support of friends and family. Gratitude comes from realizing that we can do without many of the material trappings of life, if we maintain an enlightened spiritual and psychological "center." Or, as a Yiddish proverb puts it, "If a Jew breaks a leg, he thanks God he did not break both legs. If he breaks both legs, he thanks God he did not break his neck" (modified from Gribetz 2004, 137).

That said, there are times when the mensch is entitled to "worthy discontent" (Borowitz and Schwartz 1999, 168). In fact, when we are faced with great evils—such as anti-semitism, racism, genocide, or brutality of any kind—we are *obligated* to experience "worthy discontent" and to do something constructive with that feeling! As Borowitz and Schwartz observe, "The practice of contentment must never degenerate into moral complacency. Had we been diligent early on, Hitler could have been stopped" (Borowitz and Schwartz 1999, 169).

True—but equally, let us be grateful to the bravery and sacrifice of those who ultimately *did* stop Hitler.

Barry and his girlfriend, Lynn, loved to dine in great restaurants. As two professionals with good salaries, they were able to enjoy all the finest dining spots Boston had to offer. But Barry was fussy—very fussy!—and sometimes made sarcastic remarks when everything wasn't to his liking. Sometimes he would disparage the service, sometimes the food. He rarely took notice of the relatively poor and very hard-working staff who served him and Lynn. One night, after enjoying a sumptuous main course, Barry and Lynn were not entirely pleased with the dessert. "This is unacceptable!" Barry said to the waiter. "I would expect better from a restaurant of this stature. Please let the chef know we're not happy with this dessert." The waiter did so, and the chef came out to speak with Barry and Lynn. The chef apologized and asked the couple what was wrong with the dessert. "Look," Barry said, "for the money we paid, the portion was skimpy and the pie crust was soggy." The chef again apologized and agreed not to charge the couple for the dessert. He then added, "Please don't take it out on the waiter, sir. If the dessert didn't please you, it's my fault."

Barry seems to be someone who—besides having an abrasive and obnoxious manner! (see Chapter 17)—can't seem to enjoy the bounty that he and Lynn are privileged to receive. After all, millions of people in the world go hungry each day; many starve to death. And Barry is complaining *because the pie crust is soggy?* He would do well to read the words of Ben Zoma, part of whose teaching we cited at the beginning of this chapter. Here is the complete passage from the Talmud:

> Ben Zoma...customarily said: What labors did Adam have to carry out before he obtained bread to eat? He plowed. He sowed. He reaped. He bound the sheaves, threshed the grain, winnowed the chaff, selected the ears, ground them, sifted the flour, kneaded the dough, and baked it. Only then was he able to eat. I, on the other hand, get up and find that all these things have already been done for me. Similarly, how many labors did Adam have to carry out before he obtained a garment to wear? He had to shear the sheep, wash the wool, comb it, spin it, and weave it. Then did he have a garment to wear. All I have to do is get up and find that these things too have been done for me (Berakhot 58a; in Dorff 1995, 102–3).

One wonders whether Barry's snide attitude might change if, each time he dined out with Lynn, he thought about the farmers who grew the fruit that went into his pie; the truckers who transported the fruit to the restaurant; the chef who prepared his meal; the underpaid waiter who served it; and so on. As Rabbi Dorff points out, "it is not only God whom we should thank; we also need to express our gratitude to people who do good things for us" (Dorff 1995, 102).

In this regard, we are reminded of Albert Einstein's comment, "A hundred times a day I remind myself that my inner and outer life depend on the labors of other men, living and dead, and that I must exert myself in order to give in the measure as I have received and am still receiving" (QuoteWorld.org, n.d.).

In short: it is the mark of the mensch both to *be* thankful and to *express* thanks!

PERSONAL ENCOUNTER: BEN ZOMA
AND THE GRATEFUL GUEST

Simeon ben Zoma (ca. 90–125 C.E.) was never ordained, yet he is referred to as "Rabbi" twice in the Talmud (Bader 1988, 300)—no doubt, a mark of the high esteem in which he was held by his colleagues. Known as a brilliant but obsessive scholar, ben Zoma met a sad fate: he is said to have gone mad, after having entered the "Garden of Knowledge" and being overwhelmed by the confounding visions he encountered there (Bader 1988, 300). Ben Zoma is perhaps best known for his maxim, "Who is wise? He who learns from every man! Who is strong? He who conquers his passions! Who is rich [contented]? He who is satisfied with his portion!" (Pirke Avot 4:1; cited in Bader 1988, 301).

Ben Zoma left us with a mishnah (Berakhot 58a) that, some say, describes the proper attitude of man toward God (Bader 1988, 302), who created such bounty and abundance for us to enjoy. But the passage can also be seen in a more mundane light, reflecting the attitude of two types of "guests": one grateful, the other (like Barry), snide and ungrateful:

> Ben Zoma used to say: What does a good guest say? He says: Look how much trouble my host has taken for me! How much meat he has set before me! How much wine he has set before me! How many cakes he has set before me! All the trouble he took to prepare this meal he did only for my sake. But what does a bad guest say? He says: What trouble did my host go to for me? Did he serve wine, meat, or cake? And besides, whatever trouble he did take was only for the sake of his wife and children! (cited in ibn Chaviv 1999, 55).

Each day we greet the world and the bounty it provides us—often, with so little effort on our part—we should remember to behave like a "good guest" in this life!

Chapter Seventeen

Politeness and Tact

Shammai says: Make your Torah study a fixed duty, say little and do much, and greet all people with a cheerful countenance."

—Pirke Avot 1:15

With good manners, you can open any door.

—Yiddish proverb; cited in Borowitz and Schwartz 1999, 56

One should never enter a friend's house suddenly.

—Derkh Eretz Rabbah 5.2; cited in Borowitz and Schwartz 1999, 56

R. Eleazar b. Jacob said: A person who uses rough language is like a pipe spewing foul odors in a beautiful room.

—Derkh Eretz Rabbah 3.3; cited in Borowitz and Schwartz 1999, 61

A fool utters all [that is on] his mind: but a wise man keeps it in till afterwards.

—Proverbs 29:11 (American King James Version)

Rabbi Shimon the son of Elazar says: Do not try to assuage the anger of your friend in the height of your friend's anger; do not try to comfort your friend when your friend's deceased lies before him; do not question your friend at the time your friend makes a vow; and do not seek to see your friend in the time of your friend's humiliation.

—Pirke Avot 4:23

We have already discussed (in Chapter 9) the rabbinical prohibition against shaming another in public ("Whoever shames another in public is like one who sheds blood" [Bava Metzia 58b; cited in Elkins 2007, 20]). In the present chapter, we delve a bit into the finer points of *politeness and tact*, which hold a place of honor in the rabbinical tradition—sometimes even trumping expressions of "truth." As Rabbi Elliot Dorff succinctly puts it, "When there is no practical purpose requiring the truth, and those hearing it will only have their feelings hurt, the Rabbis tell us to choose tact over truth, especially when the truth is matter of judgment in the first place" (Dorff 1995, 92).

The topic of "politeness" or "good manners" is often trivialized nowadays—reduced to learning how to "RSVP" to a dinner invitation or how much to tip the newspaper boy for the holidays. The Rabbis knew better. They realized that politeness, tact, and affability fundamentally involve *consideration for the feelings of others* and *the maintenance of harmony within the community*.

To be sure, there are practical benefits derived from appearing cheerful, even when one is not necessarily feeling all that chipper. Rabbi Dr. Abraham Twerski recounts an episode at a medical conference, where he encountered a doctor who literally used his fingers to form his mouth into a smile! "This is not a neurotic tic," the doctor explained to Rabbi Twerski. "I came across an article which said that not only does the emotion of a smile lift your spirits, but even the muscular action involved in forming a smile can make you feel better" (Twerski 1999, 61). Indeed, Rabbi Twerski observes that, "While life is a serious business, a cheerful attitude can enable us to cope much more effectively" (Twerski 1999, 61).

A smile, however, has more than a utilitarian rationale. For the Rabbis of the Talmud, the matter of *greeting others cheerfully* (Pirke Avot 1:15) was a moral responsibility, as Rabbi Reuven Bulka notes: "you may have a chip on the shoulder from what you perceive has been denied to you. Nevertheless, it is up to you not to spread your melancholy to others...[therefore] receive all people with cheerfulness" (Bulka 1993, 123).

Citing the teachings of the great rabbinical scholar, Rabbi Jacob Kamenetzky (as recollected by Rabbi Berel Wein), Rabbi Telushkin has this to say about simple courtesy: "Everybody deserves a thank-you: the waitress who serves you, the bank teller who completes your transaction, and the taxi driver who delivers you to your destination. We might be in a hurry, but saying "thank you" won't delay us" (Telushkin 2000, 90).

Borowitz and Schwartz discuss "manners, courtesy and etiquette" under the rubric of the Hebrew term, *derekh eretz* (Borowitz and Schwartz 1999, 53–65). Though this term is variously translated, in this context, it means roughly, "common decency" and "respecting the social conventions of the community." Put in very concrete terms, "If we have *derekh eretz* we're polite and affable and don't go around bumping into others, either physically or emotionally" (Borowitz and Schwartz 1999, 56). Borowitz and Schwartz draw their teachings mainly from two lesser known tractates of the Talmud, *Derekh Eretz Rabba* (D.E.R.) and *Derekh Eretz Zuta* (D.E.Z.).

Al was really miffed. He and his wife, Marge, had been neighbors of George and Kathy for fifteen years, and had gradually become good friends with the couple. Sometimes Al, Marge, George, and Kathy would go out to the movies or a ballgame together. Their children went to the same school and often played together. But when George failed to return Al's riding lawnmower— which Al had loaned George more than a month ago—Al was understandably annoyed. "Can you believe that guy?" Al said to Marge. "He's had that mower for a month now, and I've asked him twice to bring it back! He keeps telling me he'll bring it right away and then he just disappears for a few days. What the hell is wrong with him?"

Marge urged restraint. "Well, maybe he's been sick. Or, maybe he's got his mind on other things, Al. It's a little odd, actually. I haven't heard anything from Kathy in over a month, and she usually calls at least once a week. Anyway, honey, it's not worth getting angry about the mower." But Al would not be mollified. "I'm gonna give our good neighbor a piece of my mind," Al muttered, stalking out of the house with a deep scowl on his face.

Al arrived at George's house to find the front door slightly ajar. He yelled, "Yo, George! Get your fat butt over here!" When nobody responded, Al walked into the house and headed for the kitchen, where he and George would often share a beer. But before Al reached the kitchen, George emerged from the master bedroom with his arm around a woman Al did not recognize. "Oh, Jeez!" was all Al could say. "Oh, my God—what the hell are you doing in my house?" George replied angrily. "Sorry, George... I didn't know... I mean..." At this point, Al turned around and headed back to his house, where he told Marge what had happened. "Well," Marge said, "I hope you're happy, Al. I bet Kathy moved out on George for cheating on her—that's why I haven't heard from her. And you blunder into their home like a bull in a china shop!"

We can draw many lessons from Al's atrocious behavior. There is, of course, the matter of Al's *anger*. In Chapter 4, we learned of the Rabbis' stern admonitions against anger, which is closely linked with arrogance, pride, and rage—even with *idolatry* (Sherwin and Cohen 2001, 84). It should not be surprising that unrestrained anger is often the source of tactless and boorish behavior. Even when we are feeling irritable or down in the dumps, the Rabbis admonish us to "greet all people with a cheerful countenance" (Pirke Avot 1:15). Al not only failed to do so, he also entered George's house suddenly, and without knocking. Al did call out for George before storming inside—using a bit of "rough language"—but this is no substitute for the courtesy of knocking on a friend's or neighbor's door. Even better, the mensch tries to *call ahead* before showing up unexpectedly at someone's house. That way, we don't go around "bumping into others, either physically or emotionally" (Borowitz and Schwartz 1999, 56), or embarrassing those whom we might find in a compromising position.

Manny felt a little ambivalent about attending the dinner party at Ira and Jane's house. Manny and Ira had been friends and business partners for over a decade, and had built up a successful home-based computer "trouble shooting" service. Ira handled the "techie" aspects of the business, while Manny drummed up business and kept the books. In general, things had gone very well for the business—but late in the afternoon, on the day of the party, Manny got some bad news: a big client had called to say that he was dropping the service and switching to another firm. Manny debated whether it might be better to make some excuse and not show up for the party, but he decided "That wouldn't be fair or honest." He also debated whether he should withhold the bad news from Ira until the following day, but decided that he would be uncomfortable for the entire evening if he tried to "keep all this tsuris (trouble) to myself." So, shortly after arriving at Ira's house, Manny took Ira aside and broke the bad news to him. Ira looked stunned and grew very quiet. He thanked Manny for "giving me the straight scoop," but Ira's mood never recovered. He seemed morose at dinner, and his wife became concerned enough to take him aside and ask what was wrong. "I'll tell you what's wrong!" Ira shouted. "My noodnik business partner had to ruin the whole party by telling me how we lost our big money-maker client today, even though there's not a damn thing I can do about it tonight!"

Rachel of the "Urban Dictionary" (www.urbandictionary.com) defines a *noodnik* as someone who spreads cheer everywhere he doesn't go! Although Manny is evidently a person of honor—he did not want to deceive Ira, after all, and felt responsible to report what had happened—he is not necessarily a person of great *tact*. To be sure: if the business setback could somehow have been reversed the night of Ira's party, there might have been a rationale for Manny's giving Ira the bad news then and there. But in all likelihood, this was a situation where little or nothing could have been done to set things right that evening; the bad news could easily have waited until the next day.

Thus, Rabbi Dr. Abraham Twerski counsels, "Don't spread misery" (Twerski 1999, 133). He adds,

> We have to exercise good judgment as to when to share bad tidings with others. When this is of no constructive use, a statement found in *Proverbs*, "One who delivers bad tidings is a fool," applies. It is only when some good can come of your sharing such information with others that you should do so (Twerski 1999, 134).

It is not quite clear which statement in Proverbs Rabbi Twerski has in mind. However, very much in this same spirit are the words of English clergyman Matthew Henry (1662–1714), commenting on Proverbs 29:11 (translated as, "A fool uttereth all his mind: but a wise man keepeth it in till afterwards"):

> It is a piece of weakness to be very open: He is *a fool* who *utters all his mind*, who tells every thing he knows, and has in his mouth instantly whatever he has in his thoughts, and can keep no counsel; who, whatever is started in discourse, quickly shoots his bolt; who, when he is provoked, will say any thing that comes uppermost, whoever is reflected upon by it; who, when he is to speak of any business, will say all he thinks, and yet never thinks he says enough, whether choice or refuse, corn or chaff, pertinent or impertinent, you shall have it all… It is a piece of wisdom to be upon the reserve: *A wise man* will not *utter all his mind* at once, but will take time for a second thought, or reserve the present thought for a fitter time" (Henry 1706).

Indeed, both Rabbi Twerski and Matthew Henry are talking about *tact*—which we may define as *that sensitivity to the feelings of others which constrains unmodified honesty*. The mensch restrains her speech not only to avoid giving offense, but also to preserve harmony and tranquility among family, friends, and community. As we noted in Chapter 14, "Great is peace, seeing that for its sake, even God modified the truth" (Yevamot 65b).

Harriet and Sam were in their mid-80s and had lived full, rich lives. Harriet wrote childrens' books, while Sam was a successful chiropractor. In the past year, Sam had been diagnosed with prostate cancer, but he was being treated conservatively by his doctors and generally felt well. He was able to keep up most of his usual activities and maintained his zest for life. One night, Harriet and Sam had a few close friends over for dinner and drinks. Sam excused himself from the table to "take care of some business," his usual euphemism for going to the bathroom. When Sam didn't return after ten minutes, Harriet became concerned and went upstairs to check on Sam. To her horror, she found him unresponsive on the bathroom floor. Harriet kept her wits about her and immediately called 911; however, when the EMTs arrived just five minutes later, they pronounced Sam dead—most likely, the victim of a massive heart attack. At that point, Harriet fell to pieces. She sat on the living couch, and began weeping uncontrollably. One of her long-time friends, Madeleine, tried to comfort Harriet. She put her arm around Harriet and said, "You know, darling, maybe it was for the best. After all, with the cancer, Sam would have suffered. At least this way, he went quickly." At that point, Harriet stiffened, abruptly got up from the couch, and said to her friends, "Please, everyone, I need to be alone. You don't need to stay, I'll be OK."

In Pirke Avot 4:23, we are admonished by the Rabbis, "*do not try to comfort your friend when your friend's deceased lies before him*" This is actually an astounding bit of psychological wisdom. Thus, Rabbi Reuven Bulka notes that "condolences at the wrong time can cause...rejection of the attempts at comforting. An individual must be ready to accept the comfort. When the deceased is before the individual, there is no such readiness" (Bulka 1993, 170). Indeed, Rabbi Toperoff points out that in Jewish law, the appropriate time for comforting the bereaved is during *shiva*, the seven days of mourning that commence *after* the funeral (Toperoff 1997, 255).

Sometimes, depending on the individual, even comforting him *during* the period of mourning can be "too soon." We see this in Genesis 37, in the story of Joseph and his brothers. When Jacob finds his son's blood-spattered robe,

> Jacob rent his garments, and put sackcloth upon his loins, and mourned for his son many days. All his sons and all his daughters rose up to comfort him; but he refused to be comforted, and said, "No, I shall go down to Sheol [the underworld] to my son, mourning." Thus his father wept for him (Genesis 37:34–36).

In psychotherapy, too, timing is critical (Pies 2000). Prematurely rushing in to "comfort" an angry or grieving patient may backfire. As psychotherapist Thomas Moore notes, "Sometimes people need to withdraw and show their coldness. As friends and counselors, we could provide the emotional space for such feelings, without trying to change them or interpret them" (Moore 1992, 147). We see this sensitivity depicted in the book of *Job* (see Telushkin 1994, 263). When Job's children died, his three closest friends came to visit him: "And they sat with him on the ground seven days and seven nights, and *no one spoke a word to him*, for they saw that his suffering was very great" (Job, 2:13 italics added).

Indeed, sometimes the mensch shows his tact simply by sitting in silence. For as the Rabbis tell us, sometimes "there is nothing better…than silence" (Pirke Avot 1:17). Undoubtedly, Madeleine tried to comfort Harriet with the very best of intentions, but her attempt was both premature and misguided.

The death of a loved one is not made more bearable by pointing out to the survivors the "advantages" of the death (*"You know, darling, maybe it was for the best."*), and surely not when the deceased is still lying before his spouse! We conclude with some wise counsel from Maimonides. In his *Eight Chapters*, Rambam advises us that "in all of his conversations, a man should speak only about what is useful for his soul, or about what wards off harm from his soul or body, or about knowledge or virtue, or to praise virtue or a virtuous man, or to censure vice or a vicious man" (Weiss and Butterworth 1983, 76–77).

PERSONAL ENCOUNTER: RAVA AND A MATTER OF TACT

Rava lived from about 270–350 C.E., and is known as one of greatest Torah scholars of the Academy at Pumbeditha, in Babylonia. Rava was a strong proponent of combining Torah study with *proper behavior*—it is not enough merely to read about ethical actions, one must also "walk the walk" (Orthodox Union, n.d.). Rava taught that honesty is the best policy ("When one is brought for his Heavenly Judgment, the first question he is asked is, 'Did you deal honestly with your fellow human beings?' " [Shabbat 31a]), but he also understood the importance of *tact.*

Rabbi Joseph Telushkin relates a story involving Rava and one of his colleagues, Rabbi Safra. The two rabbis were walking on the outskirts of a town when they happened to run into Mar Zutra, a distinguished colleague. Believing that Rava and Rabbi Safra had come to visit him, Mar Zutra asked the two why they had gone to all that trouble, just to meet him. Rabbi Safra replied, "We did not know that you were coming; had we known it, we would have come an even greater distance." Later, Rava chastised his colleague for speaking with such frankness to Mar Zutra, fearing that this had embarrassed the great scholar. Rabbi Safra replied, "But if I hadn't told [Mar Zutra the truth], we would have been deceiving him." Rava answered, "No, he would have deceived himself" (Hullin 94b, summarized in Telushkin 2000, 41–42).

As Rabbi Telushkin puts it, "our interactions should be tactful but honest" (Telushkin 2000, 42). And sometimes, our interactions should not be excessively honest!

Chapter Eighteen

Honoring and Revering Parents and Teachers

Honor your father and mother...

—Exodus 20:12 [Fifth Commandment]

Let each of you revere his mother and father.

—Leviticus 19:3

It is an honor for children to dwell with their father, and it is an honor for the father to dwell with his children

—Exodus Rabbah 34:3; cited in Dorff 2005, 188

They asked Rabbi Eleazar, "What is the limit for honoring one's father and mother?" He said, "To the point where the parent takes [his or her child's] wallet or money and throws it in the ocean, and his child does not rebuke him."

—Babylonian Talmud, Kiddushin 32a; cited in Dorff 1995, 195

Rabbi Elazar the son of Shammua says: Let the honor of your disciple be as dear to you as your own, the honor of your colleague as dear as the reverence for your teacher, and the reverence for your teacher as dear as the awe of Heaven.

—Pirke Avot 4:15

The wise person does not speak before one who is greater in wisdom and experience

—Pirke Avot 5:10

Kibbud Av Va-em—"honor due to parents"—occupies a central position in Judaic and rabbinical ethics. The Fifth Commandment, usually stated as *"Honor your father and mother,"* is actually problematic in the rabbinical literature. The complete commandment states, "Honor your father and mother, *that you may long endure on the land which the Lord your God is giving you*" (Exodus 20:12, Deuteronomy 5:16; cited in Sherwin and Cohen 2001, 163). Rabbis Sherwin and Cohen note that the Fifth Commandment differs from the other nine, because only the fifth provides a rationale for following it; i.e., "the reason for observance is the promise of longevity and the threat of a curtailed life for non-observance" (Sherwin and Cohen 2001, 163). But for some Jewish scholars, this apparently self-serving reason for observance is troubling:

> It was inconceivable to them that one should honor one's parents merely because it would help one achieve longevity. Indeed, honoring parents, they observed, should be aimed primarily at increasing the longevity of the parent, and not of the child (Sherwin and Cohen 2001, 163–4).

Sherwin and Cohen discuss many rabbinical objections to the "self-serving" aspect of this commandment. One of these holds that honoring one's parents ought to be "natural," proceeding from the child's gratitude for his parents' love and nurturance. But the 17th century commentator, Moses Hafetz, argued that honoring one's parents is far from "natural," particularly if the parent happens to be "foolish, senile, or...incompetent" (Sherwin and Cohen 2001, 164). Indeed, a modern-day psychologist, steeped in Freud's Oedipal complex, might even add, "If anything comes naturally to a child, it is strife and competition with one's father or mother!" It is therefore understandable that, from Hafetz's standpoint, "it is...necessary for honoring parents to be specifically commanded" (Sherwin and Cohen 2001, 165).

Rabbinical debates notwithstanding, the average adult probably appreciates that showing respect and reverence toward one's parents is not always an easy task. A parent need not be "foolish, senile, or incompetent" in order to get under a daughter's skin, or to drive a son to distraction. (The opposite is often true as well, of course!) When problems arise between parents and children, it takes a "mensch" to remain respectful, if not reverential, of one's parents. And without such respect, some medieval scholars held, the very fabric of society would be torn asunder.

The Talmud makes clear that children must honor their parents not only through action, but throught *attitude*. Sherwin and Cohen relate a story from the Talmud, involving a man who fed his father pheasant. When his father asked his son how he could afford such a delicacy, the son replied, "What business is it of yours, old man? Just grind your teeth and eat in quiet like a dog" (Sherwin and Cohen 2001, 165). A mensch, of course, would never even contemplate engaging in such cruelty. Yet in subtle ways, most children often fall short of the mitzvah: *"Let each of you revere his mother and father"* (Leviticus 19:3).

Harriet, a 55–year-old attorney, was at her wit's end. For five years now, she had been flying back and forth to Florida to care for her 87–year-old father, George, who was in the late stages of Alzheimer's Disease. Harriet's mother had died several years ago, and her father was now totally dependent on his 24-hour nursing care. Harriet—an only child—had done everything she could to keep her father out of a nursing home, and he had steadfastly refused to leave his home near Sarasota, where he had lived for more than forty years. Although the nurses did their best, George was "a real handful" as one of the nurses put it. At times, he would yell at the top of his lungs, throw his food tray at the nurses, or accuse them of "poisoning" his food. He was still ambulatory, and would often wander out of his apartment, despite attempts to cajole or even physically restrain him. Harriet was torn: should she "move" her father against his will—either to her own home in New York, or to a nursing home? Harriet's husband, Phil, was not opposed to George's living with the two of them, but he was also not pleased with the idea. As a family physician, Phil was well acquainted with the problems facing families caring for a loved one with severe dementia, and he had generally discouraged Harriet from the idea of taking in her father. "Even with 24–hour nursing, he may be just too much for us to handle," Phil had said. Harriet suspected that Phil was right, but felt terribly conflicted. "We are supposed to honor our parents!" Harriet once shouted at Phil. "How can I do that if I leave him behind in Sarasota, or put him in some crummy nursing home?"

The Midrash tells us, *"It is an honor for children to dwell with their father, and it is an honor for the father to dwell with his children"* (Exodus Rabbah 34:3, cited in Dorff 2005, 188). What does this teaching mean? The full context of the teaching is that of *honoring God*: "You are My children, and I am your Father" the teaching begins. Just as we must make our home a place where God, our Father, can reside, we must also invite our earthly father (and mother) to dwell with us, in our own home.

But, as Rabbi Elliot Dorff notes, this teaching "raises questions in our day about placing elderly parents in nursing homes" (in Dorff 2005, 188). This was certainly a hot-button issue for Harriet and Phil. When our parents are severely incapacitated or suffering from dementia ("senility"), the dilemma of what the children should do becomes all the more acute. As Rabbi Joseph Telushkin tells us, "Jewish law rules that children are obligated to try to take care of a senile parent for as long as possible. Only when it is no longer possible should a child hire others to do so" (Telushkin 2000, 346).

Indeed, to behave as "menschen," we must extend our patience and endurance as far as we can when a parent has become demented, even when it means tolerating difficult or disturbing behaviors. Thus, in his *Mishneh Torah*, Maimonides tells us,

> If one's father or mother becomes mentally disordered, [the child] should try to indulge the vagaries of the stricken parent, until he [or she] is pitied by God [and dies]. But if he finds he cannot endure the situation because of the parent's madness, let him leave and go away, and appoint others to care for the parent properly (cited in Telushkin 2000, 347).

Rabbi Telushkin adds, "As for sending a parent to live in an old age home, this should be a final step, never a first one" (Telushkin 2000, 347).

Pete had joined his father's accounting firm with some reluctance. Having just earned his M.B.A., Pete's first inclination was to work for a large firm, far from home. But Pete's father had pushed him hard to "help out your old man" and had promised Pete an opportunity to "make some big bucks quickly." Since Pete was in considerable debt from loans he had taken out during college and business school, he ultimately acceded to his father's wishes. Things went reasonably well for the first six months or so, and Pete found himself pleased with both his work and salary. But one day, while preparing the tax returns for a major corporate client, Pete was surprised when his father came into his office and closed the door. "This software company is a real cash cow for our firm, Pete," his father told him. "It wouldn't hurt to be a little, you know, 'creative' when it comes to their deductions." Pete's father went on to detail some ways Pete might "creatively interpret" the tax code so as to favor the corporate client. Pete grew more and more uneasy as he heard what sounded like some very questionable, if not illegal, accounting practices. But Pete loved and respected his father, and did not want to go against his wishes. With some trepidation, Pete followed his father's instructions and prepared a very dubious tax return for the "cash cow" client.

How far are children required to go, in "honoring" their parents' wishes? Rabbi Eleazar was asked this question, and replied, "*To the point where the parent takes [his or her child's] wallet or money and throws it in the ocean, and his child does not rebuke him*" (Babylonian Talmud, Kiddushin 32a; cited in Dorff 1995, 195). In a comment on this section of the Talmud, Rabbenu Yitzhak (1115–1184) maintains that "recovering one's own property takes precedence over some acts of honoring one's parents" (Dorff 1995, 195). More broadly, as Rabbi Jacob Immanuel Schochet notes, "If parents…order their child to transgress a positive or a negative command set forth in the Torah, or even a command which is of rabbinic origin, the child must disregard the order" (Schochet, n.d.).

In the above vignette, one could argue that by placing Pete in a precarious legal position, Pete's father was indirectly taking his son's "wallet" (personal and financial security) and "throwing it in the ocean." Furthermore, Pete's father was (albeit somewhat cryptically) directing his son to transgress the command set forth in the Talmud, requiring honesty in business practices ("*When a person is brought into the heavenly Court of Judgment, he is asked: 'Did you deal honestly?'*" [Shabbat 31a; in ibn Chaviv 1999, 81]). This was an instance in which a mensch would have stood up to his father and respectfully declined to "cook the books."

In what other instances should a son or daughter decline to obey a parent's wishes? Rabbi Moshe Lieber teaches us that,

> If, out of unfounded hatred, a parent commands a child not to speak with another Jew or not to forgive that person for what he did against the parent [or the child], it is forbidden to follow the parent's command, as doing so would entail violating a Torah prohibition (Lieber 1998, 122).

Similarly, as Rabbi Telushkin observes, "No parent…has the right to try to alienate his or her child from the other parent" (Telushkin 2000, 182–3).

Parental wishes must also give way when they conflict with spousal obligations. For example, the 13th century scholar Solomon Ibn Adret dealt with a case involving a woman who was living with her husband's parents. The young woman was in a state of constant tension with her mother-in-law, who was always belittling her. The wife approached Rabbi Adret and asked if she had a right to demand that she and her husband leave the home of her in-laws, notwithstanding her husband's filial obligations. Rabbi Adret affirmed that the wife's well being took precedence over her husband's obligations to his parents (Sherwin and Cohen 2001, 166–7).

Perhaps the best synopsis of these issues is provided by Rabbi Telushkin, when he writes, "As a child, you owe your parents many things: gratitude, attention…honor, and even a sense of reverence. What you don't owe your parents, however, is control of your conscience." (Telushkin 2000, 183).

Don was a young architect working under the wing of his former professor, Louis, who had recently left academia to start his own consulting firm. Louis's textbooks on architectural engineering were considered the "gold standard" in academia. Moreover, "Lou" had always been a revered figure for Don, who saw the older man as a kind of mentor and father-figure. Don's own father had died suddenly when Don was in high school, and in many ways, Lou had stepped into the void in Don's psychological life. Over the past two years, however, Don had noticed that Lou—now in his 70s—occasionally made minor errors in some of his architectural calculations. On an important project they were doing together, Don became alarmed when he found a very subtle but potentially dangerous error in one of Lou's calculations, involving the structural supports for a large balcony. Don became convinced that the balcony, as designed, might actually collapse under certain unusual conditions. But Don felt "deeply conflicted" about what to do. "How am I supposed to tell the man who literally 'wrote the book'—my teacher and mentor—that he made a potentially dangerous error? Me, his student, still wet behind the ears!"

From the Talmudic perspective, Don's reverence for his teacher is quite laudable. Questioning one's rabbi or teacher, after all, is nothing to take lightly. The Talmud cautions us that, *"The wise person does not speak before one who is greater in wisdom and experience"* (Pirke Avot 5:10). Indeed, we are taught to hold *"the reverence for your teacher as dear as the awe of Heaven"* (Pirke Avot 4:15). Rabbi Reuven Bulka goes on to explain that

> the teacher, who is the source of an individual's knowledge, is acting on God's behalf—God being the source of all knowledge—in transmitting God's word to the individual. It is vital that the individual have as much reverence for the teacher as one is in awe of Heaven" (Bulka 1993, 161).

Just so. But, on the other hand, we find this cautionary note in the Hasidic tradition: Rabbi Moshe of Kobrin described the awe and trepidation that the great Maggid of Mezeritch felt for his teacher, the Baal Shem Tov. It was of such magnitude that when he discovered a handkerchief with a pinch of snuff on it that had belonged to his late master, he fainted! Nevertheless, he never allowed his great reverence for the Baal Shem Tov to interfere with his fear of God (Lieber 1995, 258).

In Don's case, the "fear of God" might well enter Don's heart, given that Lou's mistake could conceivably lead to injury or even death. So, what does the mensch do in such a situation? Of course, there is no way to justify ignoring such a potentially dangerous error on the part of one's mentor or teacher. As we saw in Chapter 9, the Talmudic principle of *pikuach nefesh* ("danger to life") overrides all religious laws except those involving murder, idolatry, and prohibited sexual unions (Kottek 1997, 25). And we are also told in *Tanakh*, "Don't put a stumbling block in front of a blind man" (Leviticus 19:14). One could argue that by failing to confront his teacher's error, Don would be putting up *two* stumbling blocks: one that could cost his teacher his reputation and career; and another that might cause an innocent person to lose life or limb.

Indeed, the Talmud specifically teaches as follows:

> How do we know that a disciple sitting before his master [and seeing] that the poor man is right [in a legal dispute which his teacher is adjudicating] and the wealthy man wrong, should not remain silent? Because [the Torah teaches]: "Keep far away from falsehood" (Babylonian Talmud, Shevuout 31a, in Telushkin 2000, 370–1).

As Rabbi Joseph Telushkin comments,

> Jewish ethics teaches that you do not have the right to remain silent when another person will suffer because of your silence. Thus, in… [a case] in which a teacher incorrectly favors a rich litigant, the student is required to speak up. Indeed, for the student not to do so is to commit perhaps a greater offense than the teacher's since the teacher's error is probably innocent, while the student's silence is not (Telushkin 2000, 371).

Very well, then: the mensch needs to confront even a revered teacher's error, if it is one of great moment. But how does the student do so respectfully and in a way that will not humiliate the teacher? The Talmud gives us a reasonably clear answer:

> [Rav Yehuda disagreed with his father and told him that he was wrong. Thereupon] Shmuel said to Rav Yehuda: "You brilliant scholar! Don't speak to your father that way [telling him bluntly that he made a mistake, because you embarrass him]." And so we learned in a Baraita: If a son saw his father [unintentionally] transgressing a law of the Torah, he should not say to him, "Father, you have violated a Torah law."…He should tell him calmly, "Father, it says in the Torah as follows…" [and the father will draw his own conclusion] (ibn Chaviv 1999, 636).

And so, Don might very well sit down with his mentor, Lou, and say something like, "Lou, I'm confused. I'm looking at this equation for the balcony and I don't understand. Can you help me? I thought that when this much weight needs to be supported, it requires…" etc., and allow his teacher to draw the right conclusion.

PERSONAL ENCOUNTER: RABBI TARFON
AND HIS MOTHER

Rabbi Tarfon was a member of the third generation of the Mishnah sages, living in the period of roughly 70 C.E. and 135 C.E. He is well known for his teaching, in Pirke Avot (2:20), "The day is short, the task is great, the workers are lazy, and [the] reward is great, and the Master of the house is insistent." Rabbi Tarfon was also known for his halachic disagreements with Rabbi Akiva. One of the most memorable aspects of Rabbi Tarfon's life is the great reverence he showed his mother. But even this degree of honor was recognized as inadequate by Rabbi Tarfon's colleagues! The following story is told of R. Tarfon:

> Rabbi Tarfon had an elderly mother; and whenever she wanted to go to bed he would bend down, and she would climb into bed by stepping on him; and whenever she wanted to climb out of bed, she stepped on him. He went into the bet midrash and praised [the fact that he was able to fulfill the mitzvah of honoring his mother in such a manner]. They said to him: You did not even reach half of what the mitzvah of honoring parents requires of you (Kiddushin 31b; in ibn Chaviv 1999, 494).

Afterword

We began this book by focusing on the concept of *ratzon*, which Borowitz and Schwartz defined in terms of several inter-related traits: for example, *being congenial; cultivating an easy-going nature; showing good will to others; being amiable; speaking gently to others;* and *being accommodating and conciliatory.* Most of the material we have covered was essentially an elaboration on these traits. In contrast, we have not dwelt much on the concept of "abstinence" in this book, though we did discuss the related concept of "self-mastery" in Chapter 4. Perhaps, then, we should end our discussion of the mensch by noting that *abstinence* figures prominently in the ethical writings of the 11th century sage, Bachya ibn Pakudah, author of the classic work, *The Duties of the Heart.* For ibn Pakudah, all the "duties of the heart" came down to one or another form of "abstaining"; for example, not reflexively asserting one's own needs and wishes over those of others, and not insisting on having more than one's fair share.

What does this have to do with *ratzon*? In a sense, we can think of *ratzon* as the "marriage" of two underlying dispositions: *kindness* and *abstinence.* Indeed, if forced to condense the principles of this book into one sentence, I would be inclined to say, "The mensch is someone whose character constantly reflects the two traits of *kindness* and *abstinence.*" This means living out a kind of "dialectic": kindness is a reaching out of the self; abstinence, a kind of "holding back." Like exhalation and inhalation, kindness and abstinence compose the essential dyad of moral and humane behavior. Perhaps it is fair to say that for the fully realized mensch, these traits eventually become so ingrained and instinctive, they are akin to breathing out and breathing in.

Most of us will fall short of achieving this kind of instinctual, almost bodily goodness, at least from time to time. But a real mensch will continually strive in the direction of kindness and abstinence, and—after falling short—will get up off the ground and try again.

Lexington, April, 2010

Appendix One

Selective Chronology of Sages*
and Principal Events in Land of Israel

Table A.1.1. Pre-Tannaitic and Tannaitic Period

Approximate Dates	Name of Sages	Contemporaneous Events
30 B.C.E–20 C.E.	Hillel Shammai	Herod's rule
40 C.E.–80 C.E.	Yohanan ben Zakkai	Destruction of the Second Temple (70 C.E.)
80 C.E.–110 C.E.	Eliezer ben Hyrcanus Yehoshua ben Hananiah Elisha ben Avuya (Aher)	
110 C.E.–135 C.E.	Akiva	Bar Kochba revolt (132 C.E.–135 C.E.)
135 C.E.–170 C.E.	Shimon ben Gamliel II	
170 C.E.–200 C.E.	Yehuda Ha-Nasi (Rebbi)	Final redaction of the Mishnah

Table A.1.2. Amoraic Period

Approximate Dates	Name of Sages	Contemporaneous Events
175 C.E.–247 C.E.	Rav [Abba Arika]	Sassanid Kingdom in Babylonia
220 C.E.–250 C.E.	Shmuel	
250 C.E.–290 C.E.	Yohanan Resh Lakish	
320 C.E.–350 C.E.	Abaye	Christianity officially recognized in Roman Empire
375 C.E.–425 C.E.	Rav Ashi	Development of Babylonian Talmud at Sura yeshiva

Reference: Steinsaltz 1997

*This list is far from exhaustive; rather, it represents the sages who, in the view of some scholars, have made the most significant contributions to Talmudic and rabbinical commentary.

Appendix Two

Glossary of Terms

Aggadah—non-legal material in the Talmud, including moral aphorisms and folklore

Akhzari—cruel (e.g., one who refuses to forgive)

Amoraim—literally, "interpreters"; sages responsible for the *Gemara*

Anava—humility

Avak lashon hara—"dust of the evil tongue"; talk that hints at something negative about a person without actually saying it

Azzut—obduracy, hard-heartedness

Baraita (pl. Baraitot)—a teaching in the Jewish oral law not incorporated in the *Mishnah*

Beth din—literally, "house of judgment"; a rabbinical court

Chabad—acrostic composed of *chochmah, binah,* and *da'at*; philosophy associated with Rabbi Schneur Zalman of Liadi (1745–1812)

Derekh eretz—literally, "the way of the land;" common decency

Emet—truth

Emunah—faith, faithfulness, trustworthiness

Erekh apayim—slow to anger

Gemara—Commentary on the *Mishnah*

Gemilut hasadim—acts of loving-kindness

Hakarat hatov—gratitude

Halakha—Jewish law; the legal material in the Talmud

Hatzlachah—success (either material or spiritual)

Hekhsher Tzadek—justice certification; certification of food produced so as to protect rights of workers and animals

Histapkut—contentedness

Kibbud Av Va-em—literally, honoring father and mother; honor due to parents

K'vod habriyot—human dignity or respect for persons

Lashon hara—literally, "the evil tongue"; more technically, any *true* statement that reduces the stature of the person about whom it is said
Lifnim meshurat hadin—going beyond the letter of the law
L'toeles—in service of a constructive purpose
Luftmensch—an impractical contemplative person having no definite business or income
Luftkopf—a person with his "head in the clouds"
Matanos l'evyonim—gifts to the poor (especially, on Purim)
Mechilah—forgiveness
Mensch—a decent, honorable, and caring human being
Menschlichkeit—The quality or state of being a mensch
Mishnah—the first portion of the Talmud, as established under the *Tannaim* (ca. 70–200 CE)
Mitzvah—a commandment or rabbinical directive; more loosely, an act of kindness
Modeh ani—prayer of thankfulness recited upon awakening
Motzi shem ra—literally, "giving another a bad name"; more technically, derogatory *and false* statements about someone [cf. *lashon hara*]
Nedivut—generosity
Nekimah—revenge
Netirah—bearing a grudge
Nogea B'Davar—being an interested party; having a conflict of interest
Ona'at devarim—oppressive speech; speech that induces guilt or bad feelings, or that misleads another
Peshara—arbitration of a claim in civil court
Pikuach nefesh—danger to life
Pirkei Avos—the only tractate in the Talmud (*Mishnah*) dealing exclusively with ethical teachings and maxims; part of the order *Nezikin* ("Damages")
Rahamim—the quality of kindness and compassion
Ratzon—the quality of being congenial, easy-going, and conciliatory
Rechilus—information that potentially can cause ill will between persons; potentially harmful gossip which may nevertheless reflect reality
Sechel—roughly, deep understanding combined with practical "street smarts"
Shalom bayit—literally, "peace at home"; household harmony
Shemirat haguf—taking care of the body
Semicha—rabbinical ordination; transmission of rabbinical authority to another
Shulchan Aruch—the Code of Jewish Law produced by Joseph Karo (1488–1575)
Sotah—woman suspected of adultery; "a woman who has gone astray"
Tannaim—the sages of the Mishnah

Tiruf hadaat—mental anguish

Tochachah—reproof or criticism

Tzedakah—often defined as "charity," but more strictly, acting justly (from *tzedek*, meaning "justice")

Tzeniut—modesty; the norms of modest behavior, attitude, and dress prescribed by the Torah

Yetzer hara—the "evil inclination"

Yetzer tov—the "good inclination"

Yishuv hadaat—a calm, settled state of mind (from *yashav,* meaning *to sit*)

References

A Kempis, Thomas. 1995. *The imitation of Christ*. Trans. Leo Sherley-Price. London: Penguin Books.

Adler, Morris. 1963. *The world of the Talmud*. New York: Schocken Books.

Aristotle. 1962. *Nichomachean ethics*. Trans. Martin Ostwald. Indianapolis: Bobbs-Merrill Publishing.

Bader, Gershom. 1988. *The encyclopedia of Talmudic sages*. Northvale: Jason Aronson.

Baron, Joseph L., ed. 1997. *A treasury of Jewish quotations*. Northvale: Jason Aronson.

BBC News. 2008. "'Anger control' key to recovery." http://news.bbc.co.uk/2/hi/health/7252415.stm. (accessed February 15, 2010).

Beliefnet. N.d. "Transition rituals." http://www.beliefnet.com/Health/Health-Support/Grief-and-Loss/2001/05/Transition-Rituals.aspx?p=2 (accessed April 20, 2010).

Besserman, Perle. 1994. *The way of the Jewish mystics*. Boston: Shambhala.

Biblical Hebrew. N.d. "*Tôwrâh* - 'instruction, teaching, guidance, law'." http://www.biblicalhebrew.com/wordstudies/torah.htm (accessed April 20, 2010).

Birnbaum, Philip. 1964. *A book of Jewish concepts*. New York: Hebrew Publishing.

Bokser, Ben Zion. 1989. *The Talmud: selected writings*. New York: Paulist Press.

Bokser, Ben Zion. 2001. *The wisdom of the Talmud*. New York: Citadel Press.

Borowitz, Eugene B., and Frances Weinman Schwartz. 1999. *The Jewish moral virtues*. Philadelphia: The Jewish Publication Society.

Bulka, Reuven P. 1993. *Chapters of the sages*. Northvale: Jason Aronson.

Bunim, Irving M. 1966. *Ethics from Sinai*, vol. 3. New York: Philipp Feldheim.

Campbell, Robin, trans. 1969. *Seneca: letters from a Stoic*. London: Penguin Books.

Cardozo, Nathan Lopes. 2004. "Universal love—is it possible?" Jerusalem: The David Cardozo Academy, http://www.cardozoschool.org/show_article.asp?article_id=405&cat_id=1&cat_name=Jewish+Thought+and+Philosophy&parent_id=1&subcat_id=45&subcat_name=Halacha (accessed April 20, 2010).

Collins, D. 2006. "Amish forgive, pray, and mourn." CBS News.com, October 4. http://www.cbsnews.com/stories/2006/10/04/national/main2059816.shtml. (accessed March 14, 2010).

Comte-Sponville, Andre. 1996. *A small treatise on the great virtues.* New York: Henry Holt & Co.

Curtis, R. Coleman. 2009. *Desire, self, mind, and the psychotherapies: Unifying psychological science and psychoanalysis.* Lanham, Md: Rowman & Littlefield.

Davis, Menachem, ed. 2002. *Ethics of the fathers, The Schottenstein edition.* Brooklyn: Mesorah Publications.

Davis, Ronald M. 2008. "Legacies in the circle of life." Opening Session of the AMA House of Delegates, Hyatt Regency, Chicago, Il., June 14, http://www.ama-assn.org/ama/pub/news/speeches/legacies-circle-life_print.html (accessed March 18, 2010).

Dayan, Brigitte. 2006. "In memorium: Rabbi Ahron Soloveichik." Jewish United Fund, http://www.juf.org/news/obit.aspx?id=10272

Dorff, Elliot. 2005. *The way into Tikkun Olam: Repairing the world.* Woodstock, Vt: Jewish Lights Publishing.

Dosick, Wayne. 1997. *Soul Judaism: dancing with God into a new era.* Woodstock, Vt: Jewish Lights Publishing.

Elkins, Dov P. 2007. *The Wisdom of Judaism.* Woodstock, Vt: Jewish Lights Publishing.

Ellis, Albert, and Robert A. Harper. 1975. *A guide to rational living.* North Hollywood: Wilshire Book Co.

Epstein, I., trans. 1948. "Introduction to Seder Zera'im." In *Contents of the Soncino Babylonian Talmud.* London: The Soncino Press, http://www.come-and-hear.com/talmud/zeraim.html (accessed March 22, 2010).

Feldman, Daniel Z. 1999. *The right and the good.* Northvale: Jason Aronson.

Finkelman, Shimon, and Yitzchak Berkowitz. 1995. *Chofetz chaim: a Lesson a day.* Brooklyn: Mesorah Publications.

Finnstrom, Kara, and Michael Cary. 2008. "Dad faces son's alleged killer; sees 'normal' youngster." CNN News.com, March 26. http://www.cnn.com/2008/US/03/26/jamielshaw.folo/index.html?iref=storysearch (accessed March 8, 2010).

Fogel, Joshua, and Hershey H. Friedman. 2008. Conflict of interest and the Talmud. *Journal of Business Ethics* 78: 237–46.

Foxbrunner, Roman A. 1993. *Habad.* Northvale: Jason Aronson.

Freedman, Binny. N.d. "Small tastings of Torah, Judaism and spirituality." http://www.isralight.org/assets/Text/RBF_chukatbalak06.html (accessed March 22, 2010).

Friedman, Hershey H., and Abraham C.Weisel. 2003. Should moral individuals ever lie? Insights from Jewish law. *Jewish Law Articles,* http://jlaw.com/Articles/hf_LyingPermissible.html (accessed March 22, 2010).

Forsythe, Jeff. 2008. "Torah gems from a Tzadik I knew: Rabbi Avraham Asher Zimmerman." http://www.shemayisrael.com/rabbiforsythe/hashkofa/gems.htm (accessed May 22, 2010).

Ginsburgh, Yitzchak. 2008. "Glossary of Kabbalah and Chassidut." Gal Einai Institute, http://www.inner.org/glossary/gloss_t.htm (accessed May 22, 2010).

Ginzberg, Louis. 2002. "Akiba ben Joseph." http://www.jewishencyclopedia.com/view.jsp?artid=1033&letter=A (accessed March 11, 2010).

Golden, Judah. 1957. *The living Talmud.* New York: Mentor Books.

Golinkin, David. 2003. Basic principles of Jewish business ethics. *Insight Israel* 3:1. Jerusalem: The Schechter Institute of Jewish Studies, http://www.schechter.edu/insightIsrael.aspx?ID=59 (accessed March 28, 2010).

Gribetz, Jessica. 2004. *Wise words: Jewish thoughts and stories through the ages.* New York: Harper Collins.

Gross, David C., and Esther R. Gross. 1992. *Jewish wisdom.* New York: Fawcett Crest.

Halkin, Abraham, and David Hartman. 1985. *Crisis and leadership: epistles of Maimonides.* Philadelphia: Jewish Publication Society of America.

Henry, Matthew. 1706. "Commentary on the whole Bible, vol. 3. Proverbs 29." Bible Study Tools, http://www.biblestudytools.com/commentaries/matthew-henry-complete/proverbs/29.html (accessed March 22, 2010).

Hertz, Joseph H. 1952. *Sayings of the fathers.* London: East and West Library.

Horrall, Andrew. 2004. Queen Victoria. Review of *Queen Victoria*, by Walter L. Arnstein. *Canadian Journal of History*, December. http://findarticles.com/p/articles/mi_qa3686/is_3_39/ai_n29149053/?tag=content;col1 (accessed May 22, 2010).

Hudson, Michael. 1998. "Guarding the tongue." http://www.angelfire.com/ca/dorseydon/gossip.html (accessed March 21, 2010).

Ibn Chaviv, Yaakov. 1999. *Ein Yaakov.* Trans. Avraham Y. Finkel. Northvale: Jason Aronson.

Jacobs, Joseph, and Eisenstein Judah Davis. "Schnorrer." Jewish Encyclopedia, http://www.jewishencyclopedia.com/view.jsp?artid=344&letter=S&search=schnorrer (accessed March 28, 2010).

Jacobs, Louis. 1999. *Oxford concise companion to the Jewish religion.* Oxford: Oxford University Press.

Jewish Virtual Library. 2010a. "Joseph Karo." American-Israeli Cooperative Enterprise, http://www.jewishvirtuallibrary.org/jsource/biography/JosephKaro.html (accessed March 28, 2010).

Jewish Virtual Library. 2010b. "Martin Buber." American-Israeli Cooperative Enterprise, http://www.jewishvirtuallibrary.org/jsource/biography/Buber.html (accessed March 13, 2010).

Katz, Michael, and Gershon Schwartz. 1997. *Swimming in the sea of Talmud.* Philadelphia: The Jewish Publication Society.

Klagsbrun, Francine. 1980. *Voices of wisdom.* Boston: Nonpareil/Godine.

Kolatch, Alfred J. 2000. *The second Jewish book of why.* Middle Village, NY: Jonathan David Publishers.

Kottek, Samuel S. 1997. The practice of medicine in the Bible and Talmud. In *Pioneers in Jewish medical ethics*, ed. Fred Rosner, 7–26. Northvale: Jason Aronson.

Kranzler, Harvey N. 1993. Maimonides' concept of mental health and mental illness. In *Moses Maimonides, physician, scientist, and philosopher*, ed. Fred Rosner and Samuel Kottek, 49–57. Northvale: Jason Aronson.

Leiberman, Shimon. 2000. "Kabbalah 101. Kabbala #18 - Center of the Earth." (October 9). http://www.aish.com/sp/k/48967211.html (accessed March 28, 2010).

Levenson, Alan T. 2000. *Modern Jewish thinkers*. Northvale: Jason Aronson.

Levine, Samuel J. 2007. "Looking beyond the mercy/justice dichotomy: reflections on the complementary roles of mercy and justice in Jewish law and tradition." *Journal of Catholic Legal Studies* 45: 455–71. http://new.stjohns.edu/media/3/3b7e3155994c44db9dccfcb4f885e8db.pdf (accessed April 18, 2010)

Lew, Alan. 2003. *This is real and you are completely unprepared: The days of awe as a journey of transformation*. New York: Little, Brown & Co.

Lieber, Moshe. 1998. *The fifth commandment: honoring parents—laws, insights, stories and ideas*. Brooklyn: Mesorah Publications.

Lieber, Moshe. 1995. *The Pirkei Avos treasury*. Brooklyn: Mesorah Publications, Ltd.

Miller, James E. 2003. *The art of listening in a healing way*. Fort Wayne: Willowgreen.

Minkin, Jacob S. 1987. *The teachings of Maimonides*. Northvale: Jason Aronson.

Moore, Thomas. 1992. *Care of the soul*. New York: HarperPerennial.

Newman, Louis I., and Samuel Spitz, eds. 1945. *The Talmudic anthology*. West Orange: Behrman House.

Olitzky, Kerry M., and Lori Forman. 1999. *Sacred intentions*. Woodstock, Vt: Jewish Lights Publishing.

Orthodox Union. N.d. "Great leaders of our people: Rava." OU.org, www.ou.org/about/judaism/rabbis/rava.htm (accessed April 20, 2010).

Oxford Annotated Bible, Revised Standard Version. 1962. New York: Oxford University Press.

Palatnik, Lori. 2000. Leah and the lesson of gratitude. http://www.aish.com/jl/etb/48945526.html (accessed March 22, 2010).

Pies, Ronald. 2000. *Ethics of the sages*. Northvale: Jason Aronson.

Pies, Ronald. 2008. *Everything has two handles*. Lanham: Hamilton Books.

Pies, Ronald. 1997. Maimonides and the origins of cognitive-behavioral therapy. *Journal of Cognitive Psychotherapy* 11: 21–36.

Preston, Julia. 2008. "Rabbis debate Kosher ethics at meat plant." *New York Times*, August 22. http://www.nytimes.com/2008/08/23/us/23kosher.html (accessed March 10, 2010).

Quint, Emanuel. 1990. *A restatement of Rabbinic civil law*, vol. 1. Northvale: Jason Aronson.

QuoteWorld.org. N.d. http://www.quoteworld.org/quotes/4224 (accessed March 22, 2010).

Reuben, Steven Carr. 1997. *Children of character*. Santa Monica: Canter & Associates.

Reuben, Steven Carr. Trustworthiness (Emunah) "Stand by your word." In *Spirituality of social responsibility: manifesting the Holy: healing ourselves and healing the world*, http://kehillatisrael.org/prayer_spiritualspace.php?id=530 (accessed March 22, 2010).

Rigler, Sarah Yoheved. 2001. "Beyond just desserts: a recipe for thanksgiving." http://www.aish.com/sp/so/48930392.html (accessed March 22, 2010).

Rosenak, Michael. 2001. *Tree of life, tree of knowledge.* Boulder: Westview Press.

Rosenberg, Shelley Kapnek. 2003. *Raising a mensch.* Philadelphia: The Jewish Publication Society.

Rosenfeld, Dovid. 2006. "The 48 ways: 1–2." Project Genesis, Inc., http://www.torah.org/learning/pirkei-avos/chapter6–61–2.html# (accessed March 13, 2010).

Rosner, Fred. 2004. Informing the patient about a fatal disease: from paternalism to autonomy—the Jewish view. *Cancer Investigation* 22: 949–53.

Schneerson, Menachem Mendel. 1995. *Toward a meaningful life.* Ed. Simon Jacobson. New York: William Morrow & Co.

Schochet, Jacob Immanuel. N.d. "Honor due to parents. When not to obey—an exception." http://www.chabad.org/library/article_cdo/aid/110110/jewish/When-Not-To-Obey-An-Exception.htm (accessed March 25, 2010).

Sherwin, Byron L., and Seymour J. Cohen. 2001. *Creating an ethical Jewish life.* Woodstock, Vt: Jewish Lights Publishing.

Sofer, D. N.d. "Rav Shlomo Zalman Auerbach ZT"L." Zichron Mordechai Web Site, http://www.tzemachdovid.org/gedolim/ravauerbach.html (accessed April 20, 2010).

Steinmetz, Chaim. N.d. "How Jewish is body piercing?" *Jewish Law Commentary,* http://jlaw.com/Commentary/piercing.html (accessed April 20, 2010).

Steinsaltz, Adin. 1997. *Talmudic images.* Northvale: Jason Aronson.

Steinsaltz, Adin. 1993. *The tales of Rabbi Nachman of Bratslav.* Northvale: Jason Aronson.

Stone, Jon R. 2006. *Routledge book of world proverbs.* New York: Routledge.

Telushkin, Joseph. 1994. *Jewish wisdom.* New York: William Morrow.

Telushkin, Joseph. 2000. *The book of Jewish values.* New York: Bell Tower.

Toperoff, Shlomo P. 1997. *Avot.* Northvale: Jason Aronson.

Tripp, Rhoda Thomas. 1970. *The international thesaurus of quotations.* New York: Thomas Crowell.

Troy, Gil. 2003. "Carrying a big stick." *The Forward* (August 1), http://www.forward.com/articles/7803 (accessed March 28, 2010).

Twerski, Abraham J. 1999. *It's not as tough as you think.* Brooklyn: Shaar Press.

Twerski, Abraham J. 2006. "Shabbos: the holiness of time." The TorahWeb Foundation, http://www.torahweb.org/torah/special/2006/dtwe_shabbos.html (accessed March 21, 2010).

Twerski, Abraham J. 2004. *Ten steps to being your best.* Brooklyn: Mesorah Publications.

Twersky, Isadore. 1972. *A Maimonides reader.* New York: Behrman House.

Unterman, Isaac. 1964. *Pirke Aboth.* New York: Twayne Publishers.

Wein, Berel. 2003. *Pirke Avos (the Birnbaum edition).* Brooklyn: Shaar Press.

Weinbach, Mendel. 2010. "Purim drinking and sleeping— Sanhedrin 22b." Internet Parsha sheet, parsha.net/shmos/TetzavePurim70.doc (accessed May 22, 2010).

Weiss, Raymond L., and Charles E. Butterworth C, eds. 1983. *Ethical writings of Maimonides.* New York: Dover Publications.

Wright, Alexei A., Baohui Zhang, Alaka Ray, Jennifer W. Mack, Elizabeth Trice, Tracy Balboni, Susan L. Mitchell, Vicki A. Jackson, Susan D. Block, Paul K. Maciejewski, and Holly P. Prigerson. 2008. Associations between end-of-life discussions, patient mental health, medical care near death, and caregiver bereavement adjustment. *Journal of the American Medical Association* 300: 1665–73.

Zlotowitz, Meir. 1989. *Pirkei Avos*. Brooklyn: Mesorah Publications.